# FREE SPEECH, FREE PRESS, and the LAW

*By Jethro K. Lieberman*

PRIVACY AND THE LAW

FREE SPEECH, FREE PRESS, AND THE LAW

# FREE SPEECH, FREE PRESS, and the LAW

## Jethro K. Lieberman

*Lothrop, Lee & Shepard Books*
*New York*

Library of Congress Cataloging in Publication Data

Lieberman, Jethro Koller.
    Free speech, free press, and the law.

    Includes index.
    SUMMARY: Fifty controversial cases decided by the Supreme Court show how the First Amendment protects freedom of speech and freedom of the press.
    1. Liberty of speech—United States—Cases—Juvenile literature.  2. Liberty of the press—United States—Cases—Juvenile literature.  3. United States. Supreme Court—Juvenile literature. [1. Liberty of speech—Cases.  2. Liberty of the press—Cases.  3. United States. Supreme Court]  I. Title.
KF4772.Z9L53        342′.73′085        79-22483
ISBN 0-688-41928-3     ISBN 0-688-51928-8 lib. bdg.

To the memory of

LILLIAN BATT KATZ

1887–1978

# CONTENTS

# 1.

# *IT'S A FREE COUNTRY!*

*It's a free country!* How many times have you heard those words, or used them yourself, without thinking too much about what they mean? Although they are four of the most important words spoken in the United States, their meaning is not all that obvious. Certainly they don't mean that things aren't costly—as we all know, inflation is making almost everything more and more expensive. And they don't mean that each of us is free to do whatever he or she wants to do; there are thousands of laws that prevent us from doing many things we might like to do and even think we ought to have a right to do.

But there are some things that we are free to do without first asking someone's permission or paying a fee or obtaining a license. And we are free to do them even if others object. These rights are our most cherished personal freedoms and they are, or should be, familiar:

FREE SPEECH: The right to express ourselves, our thoughts our beliefs, our hopes without getting permission first from some government official, and without fearing that we will be put in jail for saying the wrong things.

FREE PRESS: The right to publish and print our thoughts and opinions freely, without the official censorship that most countries impose.

FREEDOM OF RELIGION: The right to worship as we see fit,

without government support of a particular religion or suppression of ours by making it illegal.

FREEDOM OF ASSOCIATION: The right to meet with friends and associates to work toward our own goals, to object when we don't like what the government is doing, or even to try to have government officials we disapprove of thrown out.

FREEDOM OF THOUGHT AND OPINION: The right to think what we choose to think and to keep our thoughts to ourselves if we like.

Very few nations in the world recognize these rights. None interprets them more broadly than does the United States. That is due in no small part to the First Amendment to the United States Constitution. In forty-five words, the First Amendment commands the government to keep hands off these essential liberties. It says:

> Congress shall make no law respecting an establishment of religion, or prohibiting the free exercise thereof; or abridging the freedom of speech, or of the press; or the right of the people peaceably to assemble, and to petition the Government for a redress of grievances.

(The word "Congress" has been interpreted in the courts to mean any branch of federal, state, or local government.)

The First Amendment is among the most important charters of political liberty we Americans possess. Without it, government officials would be able to cover up their misdeeds and crimes, we could not be sure that the laws were being enforced, and we could not even know what kinds of laws it would be best to have, because people would be afraid to speak up about their problems and how to solve them. And it is not just government that would be affected—every aspect of life, from art to science, would be changed if we as a people did not possess these essential freedoms of expression.

Consider only this one example. The constitution of the Soviet Union "guarantees" freedom of speech and press, but it adds an important qualification that as a practical matter destroys those freedoms. It says that anyone who says anything or publishes anything that would harm the Soviet Union can be punished. What will harm the Soviet Union? The answer is: anything the people in power fear would interfere with them or their policies. During the 1930s the theories of a Russian agronomist, Trofim Denisovich Lysenko, came to prominence. He believed, wrongly, that characteristics plants acquired while growing could be inherited. His theories proved disastrous to Soviet agriculture, yet because his beliefs fit in with Russian political thinking it became virtually impossible for scientists to disagree with him in public—or even, for the most part, in private. Those who did lost funds, jobs, and sometimes their lives. Because there is no tradition of free speech and free press in the Soviet Union, this one relatively simple matter—free and informed discussion of genetics—was severely restricted, to the great detriment of the Russian people and of their leaders as well.

Today we take freedom of speech and the press too much for granted in the United States. We have not always possessed these freedoms. As we will see in the chapters that follow, freedom of speech and the press were won only through struggle. The struggle continues to this day, for the actual controversies that arise cannot be settled just by pointing to the bold words of the First Amendment. Those words express a great general truth—that people ought to be free to think and talk and publish —but they do not settle every problem.

Is it permissible for the government to punish someone who advocates during wartime that people resist the draft? May the government ban misleading advertisements? Are intimate facts of a person's private life protected from publication? May I organize a demonstration against nuclear energy in a public ball park in the middle of the seventh inning? May I ring people's doorbells seeking donations to a religious group if there is an ordinance that prohibits door-to-door sales?

Because these and many other cases that come to court involve matters of great consequence on which people often violently disagree, First Amendment cases can cause passionate, angry debate. For freedom of speech and the press means freedom not merely for the people whom you admire and agree with; more importantly, it means freedom for the people you hate and distrust. It can mean freedom for people who are saying mean and ugly things, who are advocating dangerous policies, or who are willing to tell things that many people believe ought to be kept secret. As a result, many people in the heat of the moment forget or ignore the fundamental importance of free speech and a free press in order to shut up someone whom they find obnoxious.

Because the principles of free speech and a free press are not always clear and because some people would just as soon disregard them, our fundamental freedoms stand constantly in danger, as many of the cases throughout this book demonstrate. First Amendment freedoms are not "self-enforcing": they will not be observed unless people want them to be observed. And that means that all of us must have a clear understanding of the basic principles of freedom. That is the purpose of the chapters that follow: to show through cases that have actually arisen in American history the problems and promises of freedom of speech and of the press.

# 2.

# DEFINING FREEDOM: THE TRIAL OF JOHN PETER ZENGER

In the early days, freedom of speech and the press was not the rule in America. A person might say or publish things—especially those of the greatest public concern: namely, about the conduct of the government—at the peril of being charged with the crime of "seditious libel," a legal term meaning to say things that make the government appear ridiculous or that give people reason to feel contempt for it (see Glossary, p. 152). Moreover, people were not free then, as they are now, to set up a printing shop or newspaper without first obtaining the government's permission.

The earliest press in America was established in Cambridge, Massachusetts, in 1639. In 1664, the colonial legislature forbade any press from operating except the one in Cambridge, and even that press could print only what was first approved by official censors. Similar rules sprang up in other colonies. When Benjamin Franklin at the age of sixteen became publisher of his half-brother James's paper, the *New England Courant*, he had to work around the censor, Increase Mather, who kept a watchful eye on what Franklin wrote. It was not an easy time for a publisher—as, indeed, it rarely had been ever, anywhere else.

But in 1735 an incident occurred in New York that fundamentally changed the meaning of freedom of the press. That incident was the trial of a German immigrant named John Peter

Zenger for seditious libel. Zenger was barely literate in English. He had been employed in the printery of William Bradford, the public printer of the colony (who himself had once been hauled before a jury for what he had printed when he was living in Pennsylvania). In 1733 several prominent New Yorkers helped Zenger establish his own press so that they would have an outlet in which to write in opposition to the established colonial government.

This they found it increasingly necessary to do because the royal governor of New York was stealing their property and depriving them of liberties they possessed as Englishmen. Appointed by the British Crown to rule across the ocean in the colonies, the royal governors were frequently greedy men, but the governor who came to New York in 1732, William Cosby, was the greediest of all. In fact, he had been removed from his previous post as governor of Minorca, an island then under British rule, because he had flagrantly stolen the property of a merchant. The British Government seemed to think the best way to cool down the uproar that resulted was to send him farther away. Once in New York, the forty-five-year-old governor demanded that the legislature grant him a large sum of money. A heated controversy arose, and the issue of how much money Governor Cosby was owed—and how much he had already taken from one plantation owner—went to court. When the Chief Justice of the New York Supreme Court ruled against Governor Cosby, Cosby removed the judge from the bench and appointed his own man, a thirty-year-old lawyer named James DeLancey.

Shortly thereafter, the thirty-six-year-old Zenger began to publish his New York *Weekly Journal*. Various eminent lawyers and property holders in New York contributed articles to Zenger's paper denouncing Governor Cosby and his administration. Among other things, they accused the governor of arbitrarily removing judges from the bench, of denying citizens the right to vote, and of depriving defendants of their right to jury trial—all deeds that Cosby had committed and that caused most people in the colony to hate and fear him.

Cosby understandably did not relish the attacks being made on him in Zenger's newspaper, which everyone in New York City took to reading eagerly each week. In January 1734, Chief Justice DeLancey directed a grand jury to investigate the "seditious libels" made against the governor and his administration and to indict those responsible (that is, to prosecute in court on criminal charges those who made the libels). But so intense was the feeling against Cosby that the grand jury, composed of colonists, refused to take any action. They refused again that October, when the Chief Justice repeated his demands for an indictment.

Finally, in November 1734, on orders of the governor's council, John Peter Zenger was arrested and thrown into jail. Although Zenger was only the "front" man and not the brains behind the paper, he rather than the authors was arrested because his was the only name associated with the paper. He languished in jail until his prosecution for seditious libel came to trial nearly nine months later, on August 4, 1735. During the time he remained imprisoned his wife continued to publish the paper, with impassioned articles by the distinguished—but anonymous or pseudonymous—contributors who had gotten Zenger into so much trouble. One of these was James Alexander, a leading New Yorker, an eminent lawyer, and a former attorney general of the colony. Alexander was to be Zenger's defense counsel, but Chief Justice DeLancey, fearing Alexander's skill and goaded by Cosby, refused to let the lawyer represent the defendant.

In his place Zenger's backers retained Andrew Hamilton, a Philadelphia lawyer and one of the most noted members of the bar in all the colonies. Then nearly eighty years old, he volunteered to serve without fee. Hamilton had been adviser to the family of William Penn and had held many of the most important offices in Pennsylvania; such was his fame that Chief Justice DeLancey would not dare refuse him the right to represent Zenger. But to guard against the chance that he might be excluded from the trial, Hamilton's friends did not announce his appointment as Zenger's lawyer until the day the trial began.

It was a hot day when the trial got under way at the old

City Hall building in New York. The courtroom was more stifling than usual because it was jammed with spectators who knew how important this case was. Chief Justice DeLancey and an associate justice took their seats and presided over the selection of the jury. Twelve men were quickly found to serve, and Thomas Hunt was named their foreman. The prosecutor, Richard Bradley, read the charges against Zenger, and then it was Hamilton's turn to speak for the defense.

From the start, Hamilton caused a sensation. He freely confessed that his client had printed and published the two papers in which he was charged with running seditious libels. That seemed to mean that Zenger was admitting his guilt, and prosecutor Bradley was quick to make the point. With such an admission, Bradley said, "I think the jury must find a verdict for the King" (in whose name all criminal prosecutions in the colonies were brought).

Not so, Hamilton replied. Printing and publishing are not criminal acts. To be guilty of the crime "the words themselves must be libelous, that is, *false, scandalous,* and *seditious.*"

To this, the prosecutor objected that it was not necessary for him to prove the statements about Cosby to be false. He repeated a rule of libel as it was understood at the time: "The greater the truth, the greater the libel." This sounds strange to us today. How can someone be guilty of a crime by saying something true about the government? But in those days, kings who ran governments not composed of the people themselves feared that the public would rebel against the monarchy if they were convinced that it was evil, corrupt, and selfish (which it generally was). True statements about the evils of government were more likely to stir the people up than false ones, so true libels— that is, true statements causing damage to the reputation of the rulers—were considered even worse than false ones.

Hamilton replied to Bradley's objections that he would "save Mr. Attorney the trouble." Hamilton, for Zenger, would instead prove the statements to be true. Of course, Chief Justice De-Lancey, Cosby's handpicked judge, could scarcely tolerate such a revolutionary notion in his courtroom. "You cannot be admitted, Mr. Hamilton, to give the truth of a libel in evidence," DeLancey said. "A libel is not to be justified; for it is nevertheless a libel that it is true." So saying, DeLancey refused to let Hamilton offer any testimony or other proof to the jury that what appeared in the *Weekly Journal* was really true.

If Chief Justice DeLancey had been more experienced, he might have ended the trial right then. Since Hamilton had admitted that Zenger had published the papers in question and since he would not be allowed to offer evidence concerning the truth of the statements, there was really nothing left to be done. Under the established rule it was up to the judges to determine whether the statements were libelous. There was no doubt how these judges would rule, of course, for it was DeLancey himself who had originally sought indictments for these same statements nineteen months earlier. So all DeLancey had to do was direct the jury to find a verdict for the King. But perhaps because he was young or because he was in awe of the legendary Hamilton, he did not stop the trial at this point.

That left Hamilton free to do a daring thing. He appealed over the head of the judges to the jurors themselves. The jurors, not the judges, Hamilton said, should decide both the facts and the law. "You are citizens of New York," he told the jurors; "you are really what the law supposes you to be, honest and lawful men; and . . . the facts which we offer to prove were not committed in a corner; they are notoriously known to be true; and therefore in your justice lies our safety."

Chief Justice DeLancey disagreed: "The jury [must] leave the matter of law to the court." Not so, Hamilton retorted: "I know they have the right beyond all dispute to determine both the law and the fact, and where they do not doubt of the law they ought to do so. This practice of leaving it to the judgment of the court, whether the words are libelous or not, in effect renders juries useless."

Why should the jury concern itself with the truth of the statements? In explaining this proposition, Hamilton set forth one of the most eloquent defenses of freedom of the press ever made. He began by pointing out that men in public office are not exempt from the law: they are obligated, just as citizens are, to obey the law. But it is difficult to punish officials: "Men in power are harder to be come at for wrongs they do, either to a private person, or to the public." That was especially true in the colonies, where in order to sue a government official the citizen would have to go to London to press his case in court. Few, if any, could afford to do this. What is left, then, to people who are oppressed? Hamilton asked. They could complain to the legislature; but the New York legislature was in the pocket of the governor. All that is left to a free people, Hamilton said, is the "right publicly to remonstrate the abuse of power, in the strongest terms, to put their neighbors upon their guard, against the craft or open violence of men in authority, and to assert with courage the sense they have of the blessing of liberty, the value they put upon it, and their resolution at all hazards to preserve it, as one of the greatest blessings Heaven can bestow."

Unless citizens were free from prosecution for speaking the truth, what would the right of free speech and press amount to? They would always fear that a judge would decree as libelous the words they spoke. For who can say what words someone might claim held the government up to contempt, to hatred, to ridicule? "If libel is understood in the large sense urged by [the prosecutor] there is scarcely a writing I know that may not be called a libel or scarce any person safe from being called to account as a libeler." Hamilton pointed out that less than two centuries before the Zenger trial, "a man would have been burnt as an heretic for owning such opinions in matters of religion as are publicly [written] and printed at this day." By 1734, he noted, the authorities were willing to tolerate statements considered exceedingly harmful to the public under an earlier regime. He emphasized the irony: "That in New York a man may make very free with his God, but he must take special care what he says of his governor."

Hamilton agreed that false statements condemning the government ought to be punishable, for it is important to retain public confidence in the government. But history has shown how often it is the abuse of power that has brought the government "into contempt with the people." Such, Hamilton argued, was the case before the jury. And he ended his plea to the twelve jurors with these eloquent words:

> The question before the court and you, gentlemen of the jury, is not of small nor private concern, it is not the cause of a poor printer, nor of New York alone, which you are now trying: No! It may in its consequence affect every freeman that lives under a British government on the main of America. It is the best cause. It is the cause of liberty; and I make no doubt but your upright conduct, this day, will not only entitle you to the love and esteem of your fellow-citizens; but every man who prefers freedom to a life of slavery will bless and honor you, as men who have baffled the attempt of tyranny; and by an impartial and uncorrupt verdict, have laid a noble foundation for securing to ourselves, our posterity, and our neighbors. That, to which nature and the laws of our country have given us a right— the liberty—both of exposing and opposing arbitrary power (in these parts of the world, at least) by speaking and writing Truth.

*main idea*

Chief Justice DeLancey did not let these stirring remarks go in silence. He instructed the jury, as was his obligation, that the law left the question of libel to the judge—telling the jurors, in effect, that there was only one possible verdict: Guilty.

The jurors left the courtroom to deliberate on their verdict. In a brief while they returned. The clerk of the court turned to the foreman Thomas Hunt and inquired what the verdict was. "Not guilty," Hunt shouted out, and the spectators broke into cheers which the Chief Justice could not quiet down.

They had cause to cheer. The Zenger trial established an

important precedent for the principle of a free press in America. The case made news everywhere; in 1736, several months after his acquittal, Zenger published a lengthy account of his trial, including the transcript of Andrew Hamilton's celebrated statement to the jury. Although the legislatures of several of the colonies made trouble for the few newspapers that existed in America, the royal governors kept their hands off, and by the time of the War of Independence it was generally understood that government was not to have any hand in licensing the press, nor was it to punish those who spoke the truth about the government. These notions were enshrined in the First Amendment.

For his part, Zenger continued publishing his *Weekly Journal*, now famous beyond any former expectation. He died in 1746, and Mrs. Zenger kept the paper going for five years until it finally went bankrupt in 1751. Governor Cosby himself died in 1736, the year Zenger published his account of the trial that left Americans free to criticize their government.

# 3.

## *NO PRIOR RESTRAINTS*

Basic to the First Amendment is the notion that the government is not to act as censor. Congress may not, for example, pass a law requiring newspapers to send their stories to Washington for prior approval before printing them. It is not the business of the government to inquire into what a writer wants to write, how an editor intends to edit, what a publisher decides to print, what a speaker says, or what you or I or anyone has on his mind. What is spoken and written and published is decided upon by millions of individuals every day, and we are all free to hear or read what they have to say—free, that is, of government interference.

But it is not always easy to recognize a prior restraint—that is, a law that requires prior screening or allows government to censor the contents of an article in some way before publication. A public censorship board watching over the daily doings of a newspaper is easy to spot as being unconstitutional, so except in a very few instances (see p. 106), neither the states nor the federal government have tried to establish such a thing. Threats to freedom from prior restraint are usually more subtle. Generally they come from the attempt of governments to enjoin (that is, legally prohibit) a newspaper from publishing certain articles. Two cases that went to the United States Supreme Court, one from Minnesota in 1931 and one from New York forty years later, show how prior restraints can arise. We will explore these cases in some detail.

## THE CASE OF THE SCANDALOUS NEWSPAPER

Beginning in September 1927, a man named Near, publisher of a newspaper called the *Saturday Press* in Minneapolis, Minnesota, distributed editions of his paper that were scandalous in the extreme. Angry at the mayor of Minneapolis, the chief of police, the county attorney, and certain other officials, including members of a grand jury, for what he saw as their failure to control gambling, bootlegging, and racketeering in the city, Near denounced them in strident and ugly terms in a series of articles that blamed the city's crime on "Jewish gangsters." An excerpt from one article does not make pleasant reading:

> Practically every vendor of vile hooch, every owner of a moonshine still, every snake-faced gangster and embryonic yegg in the Twin Cities is a JEW. . . . I simply state a fact when I say that ninety percent of the crimes committed against society in this city are committed by Jew gangsters. . . . It is Jew, Jew, Jew, as long as one cares to comb over the records. . . . I am launching no attack against the Jewish people AS A RACE. I am merely calling attention to a FACT. . . . Up to the present we have been merely tapping on the window. Very soon we shall start smashing glass.

A Minnesota law enacted two years earlier, in 1925, permitted the public authorities to seek an injunction (a court order) closing down any "malicious, scandalous and defamatory newspaper, magazine or other periodical" as a "public nuisance." After about eight issues of the *Saturday Press* appeared with articles on the theme of "Jewish gangsters" and charges that the public officials were either in league with them or unable to bring them to trial, the county attorney (who himself had been attacked in Near's paper) went to court and obtained an injunction against further publication of the *Saturday Press*. The trial judge's order perpetually prohibited Near and his colleagues "from producing, editing, publishing, circulating, having in their possession, selling or giving away any publication whatsoever, which is a malicious, scandalous or defamatory newspaper."

Near appealed to the Minnesota Supreme Court, saying that his First Amendment right to freedom of the press had been trampled on. The state supreme court rejected his argument, noting that under the court order he was free to publish any newspaper he wanted as long as it did not contain the scandalous material in it that the trial court had adjudged to be a "public nuisance."

This answer did not satisfy Near, for two reasons. First, it told him that he could not continue to publish the kinds of articles he had been running, and which he wanted to continue to run. Second, violation of a court injunction is punishable by a jail sentence for contempt of court. But nothing in the injunction told him where the line was drawn between permissible and impermissible articles. Suppose he moderated his intemperate tone, but continued to make the same basic points. Would such an article be a "public nuisance"? He would risk jail every time he published such an article.

So Near appealed to the Supreme Court of the United States. That Court, composed of nine justices, sits in Washington to hear appeals from cases all across the United States. Not every case may be brought to it, but one in which a litigant claims that his federal constitutional rights have been infringed may certainly be heard by the High Court.

By the close vote of 5–4, the Supreme Court agreed with Near. It reversed the decision of the Minnesota courts, voided the state law, and reaffirmed the right of every person to speak or publish without prior approval from the state.

Chief Justice Charles Evans Hughes, writing the majority opinion for the Court, began by explaining the purpose and effect of the Minnesota statute under which the county attorney had enjoined the newspaper. First, it did not alter the right of someone who felt personally injured by the articles to sue for money damages in court. Instead, the statute was "aimed at the distribution of scandalous matter 'as detrimental to public morals and to the general welfare,' tending 'to disturb the peace of the community' and 'to provoke assaults and the commission of crime.'"

Second, the statute was aimed not only at statements about private citizens but about public officials, and the law would be more likely to come into play when the articles raised serious charges about corruption and neglect of public duties. Why? Because those are precisely the kinds of charges that someone is likely to think scandalous, especially if the "someone" is a public official against whom the charges are made.

Third, the law was used not so much to punish the creator of the public nuisance as it was to shut down his newspaper.

Fourth, the effect of the law was "to put the publisher under an effective censorship." The law itself did not define what was "malicious, scandalous, or defamatory," but Near was prohibited from publishing any periodical that contained such stories. As already pointed out, Near would be running a big risk in writing about the same people or about what he saw as their dereliction of duties. He would have to prove every charge to a judge and persuade the judge that everything he wrote was published for justifiable reasons. "This is the essence of censorship."

Turning to the history of the United States, Chief Justice Hughes observed that freedom of the press was understood to mean that publishers and editors are to be free not only from royal or executive interference, but also from legislative interference in the form of a prior restraint. It was considered illegitimate for even the people themselves, through their elected representatives, to pass such laws. If such a law as Minnesota's were allowed to stand, the legislature could set up a body for determining, without any guidelines, "what are justifiable ends"; such a government group could restrain publication for any reason whatsoever. To argue that a state has the power to prevent something from being published "in order to protect the community against the circulation of charges of misconduct, and especially of official misconduct," is to argue directly for an official censor, the very thing that the Founding Fathers had written the First Amendment to guard against. So the law violated the First Amendment, and the Supreme Court declared that it was unconstitutional and could not be enforced by the Minnesota authorities. The injunction was "dissolved."

The Court's conclusion did not mean, Chief Justice Hughes wrote, that Near and his staff could not be punished *after* the articles appeared. If they were telling malicious lies about particular individuals, harming their reputations, then private lawsuits could still be brought. The only thing the Court decided in this case was that the First Amendment prohibits almost every prior governmental restraint against publication.

Notice the word "almost." Chief Justice Hughes said that "the protection even as to previous restraint is not absolutely unlimited." There are times when it might be vital to prevent certain things from being published, for once they are published the damage is already done and cannot be undone. For example, the Chief Justice explained, in wartime "no one would question but that a government might prevent actual obstruction to its recruiting service or the publication of the sailing dates of transports or the number and location of troops." It was this seeming exception to the general principle against prior restraint that led to the next important case.

### THE PENTAGON PAPERS CASE

In the late winter and early spring of 1971, an incredible set of documents came into the hands of certain reporters for the New York *Times*. The documents were forty-seven volumes of U.S. Defense Department material dealing with the history of American involvement in the Vietnam war. Much of the material was sensitive; all of it was officially classified as "top secret." In June 1967, the forty-seven volumes had been commissioned as an internal study by the then Secretary of Defense Robert S. McNamara. None of the material concerned events beyond 1968.

Most of the forty-seven volumes were "leaked" to the *Times* by a former assistant to McNamara named Daniel Ellsberg and his colleague Anthony Russo. They had grown disenchanted with the war as it lingered on; though Ellsberg originally supported the U.S. position, he finally became disgusted with what he perceived to be the government's dishonest motivation for continuing the fighting and with much of the conduct of the war itself.

Keeping their "catch" under tight wraps (much tighter, it turned out, than the security that covered the Pentagon), a few *Times* editors plowed through the thousands of pages in about three months and prepared a series of articles about the revelations contained in them. During this time the Defense Department officials had no knowledge that the *Times* had seen the study, officially known as "History of U.S. Decision-Making Process on Vietnam Policy," but shortly to be known ever after as the "Pentagon Papers."

On June 13, 1971, the *Times* began to run the series, together with excerpts from the Papers themselves. (Within a few days the Washington *Post*, which also had obtained copies of the Papers, began its own series.) The articles—and the promise of several more to come during the next week—caused a sensation and panic within the highest circles of the government, even though the government had changed hands when Richard Nixon became President in 1969 and those who were in power during the years of the study no longer held office.

Nevertheless, the Nixon Administration had supported many of the policies disclosed in the Pentagon Papers, and the Administration worried both about embarrassment to the government over specific facts revealed and about whether other governments would ever again trust the United States to keep important diplomatic secrets out of the hands of newspapers. So, for the first time in American history, the U.S. Government went to court to stop the presses.

Although the Government soon lost the case, it achieved in a way a partial victory, for when the Attorney General of the United States (the head of the Justice Department and chief legal officer of the government) went to court to seek a permanent injunction, the courts immediately forbade the newspapers from publishing until the lawsuits were resolved. The newspapers did indeed cease publication of the particular articles. For the first time, the Government had succeeded in blocking the news.

The stories about the Pentagon Papers did not stay out of print for long, however; the court orders against publication amounted to delays of about two weeks. The courts speeded up their procedures so that from the time the Supreme Court first got notice of appeal to the time it rendered its decision, only six days went by. (Normally an appeal to the Supreme Court from a lower court takes a year or more.) So great was the speed that Chief Justice Warren E. Burger complained that "these cases have been conducted in unseemly haste."

As the cases (the *Times* and *Post* were involved in separate proceedings) came to the Supreme Court, the situation stood this way: On June 18 the Justice Department had asked the U.S. District Court in New York to enjoin the *Times*; on June 21 it asked the U.S. District Court in Washington to enjoin the *Post*. On June 19 the trial judge in New York ruled against the Government. And on June 21, the same day he heard the case, the trial judge in Washington also ruled against the Government. Two U.S. Courts of Appeals considered immediate appeals from these decisions on June 22, but the next day they reached opposite conclusions. The appellate court in Washington agreed with the trial judge and refused to reverse his decision, saying that the *Post* could go to press with the articles. That same day, June 23, the appellate court in New York said it wanted the New York trial judge to obtain additional information and "remanded" it (sent the case back) to him to do so. Each appellate court issued a "stay"—an order saying that no disputed stories could be published until time to appeal to the Supreme Court had elapsed. The parties were given one day to appeal. The *Times* filed its appeal in the Supreme Court on June 24, as did the United States in the *Post* case. The Court issued its own "stay" and ordered an oral hearing on June 26. Four days later, on June 30, the Supreme Court by a 6–3 vote threw the Government out of court and said the papers were free to resume publication of their articles. Both papers continued their series the following day.

The unsigned opinion of the Court was brief. In some 250 words it said simply that the Government has a "heavy burden" to meet in trying to prevent a story from being aired in public and that the Government had not met the burden in these cases. Following this opinion, each of the nine justices wrote a separate, more personal opinion—a reflection of the passion the case had stirred up.

Justice Hugo L. Black, then the senior justice next to the Chief Justice (who was one of the dissenters in the case), charged that:

> the Executive Branch seems to have forgotten the essential purpose and history of the First Amendment. . . . In the First Amendment the Founding Fathers gave the free press the protection it must have to fulfill its essential role in our democracy. The press was to serve the governed, not the governors. The Government's power to censor the press was abolished so that the press would remain forever free to censure the Government. The press was protected so that it could bare the secrets of government and inform the people. Only a free and unrestrained press can effectively expose deception in government. And paramount among the responsibilities of a free press is the duty to prevent any part of the government from deceiving the people and sending them off to distant lands to die of foreign fevers and foreign shot and shell.

Justice Black rejected the Government's position that the President has "inherent power" to protect the national security by seeking to prevent publication of damaging news stories, both because the President is commander-in-chief of the armed forces and because under the Constitution he is empowered to conduct the foreign affairs of the nation. Said Black: "To find that the President has 'inherent power' to halt the publication of news by resort to the courts would wipe out the First Amendment and destroy the fundamental liberty and security of the very people the Government hopes to make 'secure.'"

Justice William O. Douglas agreed with Black and made another point: Congress had enacted no law that gave any support to the Government's position. No law relating to treason or espionage gave the Government any power to suppress a news story of this sort. There are provisions in federal law that make it a crime *during wartime* to publish certain specific kinds of information—like secret codes and the location of troops—but even those laws do not permit the Government to *prevent* publication. They merely permit it to punish the publisher after the story is printed. As Douglas observed:

It is common knowledge that the First Amendment was adopted against the widespread use of [the law] . . . to punish the dissemination of material that is embarrassing to the powers-that-be. The present cases will, I think, go down in history as the most dramatic illustration of that principle. A debate of large proportions goes on in the Nation over our posture in Vietnam. That debate antedated the disclosure of the contents of the present documents. The latter are highly relevant to the debate in progress. Secrecy in government is fundamentally anti-democratic, perpetuating bureaucratic errors. Open debate and discussion of public issues are vital to our national health.

Justice William Brennan said that the error the lower courts made was in even temporarily prohibiting publication. A claim that publication of the Pentagon Papers "could" or "might" or "may" prejudice the national interest is simply not strong enough to support a prior restraint, he declared.

Justice Potter Stewart noted that the only solution to the problem the government perceived was to exercise a higher degree of diligence in keeping sensitive papers secret. If the President is worried about exposing confidential documents in public, then he should keep to a minimum the number of such documents and guard them closely. That function is not for Congress or the courts to perform (as through a lawsuit such as the Pentagon Papers case).

Justice Byron R. White agreed with the majority that the Government had not met its burden, but only because of the "extraordinary protection against prior restraints enjoyed by the press under our constitutional system." White sounded a cautionary note. Having examined the papers, he could not, he said, "deny that revelation of these documents will do substantial damage to public interests." And he pointed out that lifting the ban on further publication of the Pentagon Papers "does not mean that the law either requires or invites newspapers or others to publish them or that they will be immune from criminal action if they do."

Finally, Justice Thurgood Marshall, the last of the six judges to vote against the Government, said that the basic issue was "whether this Court or the Congress has the power to make law." Pointing, as did Justice Douglas, to the absence of any law passed by Congress that would permit the Government to enjoin the press, he said "it would . . . be utterly inconsistent with the concept of separation of powers for this Court to use its power of contempt to prevent behavior that Congress has specifically declined to prohibit."

The three dissenters—Chief Justice Burger and Justices John M. Harlan and Harry A. Blackmun—made two basic points. One was that the cases were conducted with such speed that not enough of the facts were known to make a sound judgment. The second point was that if there had been more time to consider the cases, discussion by the lawyers might have let the judges see that the inherent power of the President to conduct the nation's foreign policy extends under extraordinary circumstances to stopping the presses. "Would it have been unreasonable," the Chief Justice inquired, "since the newspaper could anticipate the Government's objections to release of secret material, to give the Government an opportunity to review the entire collection and determine whether agreement could be reached on publication?" But his question appeared to assume the very point that was being debated: whether a free press has any obligation to turn over anything to the Government or to consult with it before publishing anything. The answer that the Supreme Court gave in the Pentagon Papers—and the answer that still stands—is that the press has no such obligation. Because it does not, the press is free.

But what of the point that Justice White and others made: that there may be laws punishing the press *after* publication, for disclosure of secrets? In fact, the Justice Department brought to trial Daniel Ellsberg and Anthony Russo, the two who turned the Pentagon Papers over to the *Times*, on criminal charges of stealing government property and violating security laws. The Government did not indict the newspapers for receiving stolen property, however. So the trial would not have tested the Government's power to punish for disclosure of official secrets. As it turned out, the Government did not even succeed in its attempts to imprison Ellsberg and Russo because during the course of the trial the prosecutors themselves violated the law and disregarded specific instructions of the judges in their conduct of the case, causing the trial judge to dismiss the charges against the two defendants. Ellsberg and Russo went free.

# 4.

## *CLEAR AND PRESENT DANGER*

If the First Amendment means anything, it means that we are free to speak and publish without fear of prior censorship by the government. But is that enough to guarantee liberty of speech and the press? Several justices suggested, as we have seen, that crimes may have been committed in publishing the Pentagon Papers. And in Near's case, no justice claimed that the First Amendment would shield Near from the threat of a libel suit. So although a newspaper may actually put into print whatever it likes, there may still be considerable risks in doing so. If these risks are too high, is it possible to say that we are free to speak and publish? Obviously not. For example, if Zenger could be put in jail for speaking the truth about the royal governor of New York, or someone else could be imprisoned for voicing his opinion of American involvement in a war, then there would be serious abridgments of "free" speech and press.

On the other hand, absolute freedom may be harmful. That is, if there were absolutely no risks of being punished or being sued for whatever is said or published, then people might not hesitate to incite others to riot, to publish false advertisements to "make a quick buck," to tell false things about a person's reputation in order to injure him or her, and to make nuisances of themselves in other ways to the detriment of a civilized community.

32

So even though we possess the First Amendment, lines must still be drawn between what may and may not be said or published. This and the following chapters will explore some of the ways the courts have drawn the lines. As you read through the cases you will see a general rule emerge: the more the statement —oral or written—relates to public affairs and public issues, the more likely it is to be protected. That means that accounts— whether factual or opinionated—about government, its workings and its officers, are accorded the highest protection. We are almost completely free to speak and write about political and governmental affairs without fear of censorship or punishment after the fact. But the First Amendment is not limited only to speech about the government. There are other matters that are of great concern to the public—matters of economics, of society, of morality—that are also protected. Generally speaking, only when the discussion relates to private affairs does the possibility arise that the particular speech or publication may be regulated in some manner.

In this chapter we will begin by returning to the problem that John Peter Zenger posed for his government. Zenger won his case, of course, and the principle was established that the press could not be censored nor could the publisher be tossed into jail for speaking the truth about government. But that case occurred before the First Amendment existed, and in any event Zenger's trial did not deal with the problem of opinions or false statements about the government. Cases concerning these issues cropped up later.

In fact, such cases did not arise until much later. In 1798, seven years after the First Amendment was ratified and took effect, Congress enacted (during the presidency of the Federalist John Adams), a law called the Sedition Act. This law made it criminal to "write, print, utter or publish . . . any false, scandalous and malicious writings against the government of the United States, or either house of the Congress . . . or the President of the United States, with intent to defame . . . or to bring them . . . into contempt or disrepute; or to excite against them . . . the hatred of the good people of the United States, or to stir up sedition within the United States . . ." Many people thought this law violated the First Amendment, but though there were several trials in the lower courts, no case ever came on appeal to the Supreme Court. By its own terms the law only lasted three years, and in 1801 it expired.

Not until the First World War, more than a century later, did the issues presented by the Sedition Act arise again. Then Congress enacted new laws, especially the Espionage Act of 1917. Because there was resistance to the war, several people were prosecuted for violating this Act, and some of these cases reached the Supreme Court. Let us turn to those now.

### THE DRAFT RESISTANCE CASE

The Espionage Act prohibited attempts to cause soldiers and sailors to disobey their orders. It also prohibited obstructions of government efforts to recruit civilians for military service. A man named Schenck, who was general secretary of the Socialist Party of the United States, was convicted of violating the Espionage Act for supervising the mailing out of 15,000 copies of a leaflet said to be harmful to the U.S. war effort against Germany.

On its front side the leaflet quoted the Thirteenth Amendment, which abolished slavery, and said that the federal draft law violated that amendment. A draftee, the leaflet declared, was not much better off than a convict. "Do not submit to intimidation," it said, charging that conscription into the armed services amounted to tyranny. It concluded with a petition for repeal of the draft law.

The reverse side of the leaflet was headed "Assert Your Rights." It claimed that a conspiracy of Wall Street capitalists was oppressing the people of the United States, and said that the government had no legal power to send soldiers to foreign shores to shoot and kill other peoples. The leaflet wound up: "You must do your share to maintain, support, and uphold the rights of the people of this country."

By today's standards, the leaflet was quite mild. But during the First World War, Lenin just having taken over Russia in the name of the Communist Party, there was great fear of socialist or communist efforts to interfere with the nation's conduct of the war. In 1918 Schenck's conviction was upheld by the Supreme Court, in an opinion by Justice Oliver Wendell Holmes. "When a nation is at war many things that might be said in time of peace are such a hindrance to its effort that their utterance will not be endured so long as men fight." In explaining why this is so, Justice Holmes set forth, in a famous passage, a standard for measuring free speech and press in the future. Wrote Justice Holmes:

> The character of every act depends upon the circumstances in which it is done. The most stringent protection of free speech would not protect a man in falsely shouting fire in a theater, and causing a panic. . . . The question in every case is whether the words used are used in such circumstances and are of such a nature as to create a clear and present danger that they will bring about the substantive evils that Congress has a right to prevent.

In other words, espionage laws are not unconstitutional simply because the act of committing espionage in wartime may involve the act of speaking or writing. Congress has the right to declare war, the President has the right to conduct war, and efforts to interfere with the nation's ability to wage war are evils that Congress may legislate against. Acts that present an immediate and obvious danger to the war effort may be punished. Such was the case, Justice Holmes said, of the leaflet urging people to avoid the draft.

Of course, it may seem odd that Schenck was convicted

under this "clear and present danger" standard, since it is impossible to argue that mailing out those 15,000 leaflets would actually interfere with the ability of the U.S. to recruit soldiers. But, said Holmes, no one could deny that an actual obstruction of a draft office would be punishable, and this was a "conspiracy" (an agreement between two or more persons) to do so. That the conspiracy had not succeeded was no defense.

So in the first major test of free speech under the First Amendment, free speech lost. And although it continued to lose for some years, it was Justice Holmes in a case the very next year who showed where the line ought to be drawn.

### THE CONTEMPT OF GOVERNMENT CASE

In 1919, the year after Schenck's conviction was upheld, another case came to the Supreme Court, involving the conviction of five people also for violating the Espionage Act. They published two leaflets full of intemperate words and were sentenced to twenty years' imprisonment.

In general terms, the two leaflets condemned a conspiracy between "German militarism" and American capitalism to "crush the Russian Revolution." Branding President Wilson a "coward," the leaflets declared it a crime for workers in America to fight workers in Russia and cried: "Awake! Awake, you Workers of the World! Revolutionists." One of the leaflets, addressing itself to Russian immigrants, said: "Workers in the ammunition factories, you are producing bullets, bayonets, cannon, to murder not only the Germans, but also your dearest, best, who are in Russia and are fighting for freedom." The leaflet ended with a call for a "general strike."

The Government's fear was fourfold, as expressed in its prosecution of the five writers and distributors of the leaflets. First, it charged a conspiracy to publish abusive language about the form of the government of the United States. Second, it charged a conspiracy to heap contempt on the U.S. government. Third, it charged a conspiracy to encourage resistance to the war effort. And fourth, it charged a conspiracy to goad people into curtailing production of materials—like bullets and bayonets—necessary for war.

By a 7–2 vote, the Supreme Court upheld the convictions and the twenty-year sentences. But Justice Holmes dissented in a powerful opinion. These trials, he said, were nothing more than persecutions for the expression of opinions. Those who were convicted did not have, as required by the Espionage Act, intent to cripple the United States in its ability to wage the war. These "poor and puny anonymities," as he called the defendants, were being punished only because the Administration did not like what they were saying, leading Justice Holmes to his famous protest:

> When men have realized that time has upset many fighting faiths, they may come to believe even more than they believe the very foundations of their conduct that the ultimate good desired is better reached by free trade in ideas—that the best test of truth is the power of the thought to get itself accepted in the competition of the market, and that truth is the only ground upon which their wishes safely can be carried out. That at any rate is the theory of our Constitution. It is an experiment, as all life is an experiment. Every year if not every day we have to wager our salvation upon some prophecy based upon imperfect knowledge. While that experiment is part of our system I think that we should be eternally vigilant against attempts to check the expression of opinions that we loathe and believe to be fraught with death, unless they so imminently threaten immediate interference with the lawful and pressing purposes of the law that an immediate check is required to save the country.

Justice Holmes regretted that he could not "put into more impressive words" his belief that the trial and conviction of the defendants deprived them of their First Amendment rights, but his words have come down to us as among the most impressive statements of the meaning and purpose of free speech and free press. During the course of the sixty years that have gone by since Holmes penned those sentences, they have swept aside the majority opinion in the 1919 case and come to express the prevailing rule of law.

In 1943, for example, in the only such case the Supreme Court had occasion to decide during World War II, two Jehovah's Witnesses were convicted in a Mississippi state court for violating a state statute making it criminal to teach or distribute literature aimed at encouraging violence, sabotage, or disloyalty to the United States or to Mississippi. Among the statements asserted as a violation of the law was this: "It was wrong for our President to send our boys across in uniform to fight our enemies." The Supreme Court unanimously reversed the convictions. There can be no criminal punishment for expressing one's "beliefs and opinions concerning domestic measures and trends in national and world affairs."

During the Vietnam war, the Supreme Court reaffirmed this view. Julian Bond, a young black lawyer elected to the Georgia House of Representatives, was not permitted by the House to take his seat because of statements he had made and endorsed in opposition to U.S. draft and war policies. Among the statements he had endorsed was one that read in part:

> We are in sympathy with, and support, the men in this country who are unwilling to respond to a military draft which would compel them to contribute their lives to United States aggression in Viet Nam in the name of the "freedom" we find so false in this country. . . . We believe that work in the civil rights movement and with other human relations organizations is a valid alternative to the draft. We urge all Americans

to seek this alternative, knowing full well it may cost their lives—as painfully as in Viet Nam.

Again, unanimously, the Court ruled that the First Amendment fully protects such a statement of opinion and that Georgia could not, therefore, deny Bond his seat in the House.

### GUILT BY ASSOCIATION

Scores of cases dealing with free speech in wartime have come to the courts. As we have seen, not all came out on the side of free speech. But one particularly troublesome problem arose for speech and press during the uncertain peace called the Cold War that emerged from World War II. This was the problem of the rights of persons who joined the Communist Party and other organizations that called for (or seemed to call for) the overthrow of the United States Government by force and violence.

Cases dealing with people who belonged to the Party go back to the early years of the twentieth century, when various states passed sedition laws aimed at jailing people who promoted violent overthrow of the government. As laudable as such laws may be when used against people who actually engage in violence, all too often they have been used against people who merely have expressed fundamentally different political views about the way in which government ought to be organized and exercised.

In a 1937 case, for example, Dirk De Jonge was convicted in Oregon under the state "criminal syndicalism" statute, which declared as criminal behavior the advocacy of violent or unlawful means to cause political change. Included within the statute's definition of "unlawful means" were the printing and distributing of books advocating "criminal syndicalism" and the organization and presiding at meetings of groups dedicated to the idea.

De Jonge was a member of the Communist Party and presided at a meeting called by a branch of the Party in Oregon to protest the police shooting of longshoremen while on strike in Portland. The meeting itself was orderly and was attended by between 150 and 300 people. At most, fifty were members of the Party. Solely because he had presided at the meeting, De Jonge was convicted and sentenced to seven years in jail.

The Supreme Court reversed the conviction. In an opinion by Chief Justice Hughes, the Court said it recognized that First Amendment "rights may be abused by using speech or press or assembly in order to incite to violence and crime," and legislatures may pass laws against the abuse. But such laws can deal only with the abuse:

> The rights themselves must not be curtailed. The greater the importance of safeguarding the community from incitements to the overthrow of our institutions by force and violence, the more imperative is the need to preserve inviolate the constitutional rights of free speech, free press and free assembly in order to maintain the opportunity for free political discussion, to the end that government may be responsive to the will of the people and that changes, if desired, may be obtained by peaceful means. Therein lies the security of the Republic, the very foundation of constitutional government.

The Court ruled that "peaceable assembly for lawful discussion" cannot be made a crime, no matter who the people are or what party they belong to.

Three years after De Jonge's conviction was overturned, in 1940, Congress enacted the so-called Smith Act. This law makes punishable by a term of up to twenty years in prison the teaching or advising of the duty or desirability of overthrowing the government by force and violence. The same penalties apply to any person who organizes or helps to organize a group of persons with those same goals. The law also applies to a member of such groups if it can be shown that he or she is aware of the purposes of the group. The Smith Act was aimed at the Communist Party. During the 1920s and 1930s many people thought the Party posed a threat to the internal security of the nation. Ironically, it was not then unlawful to be a member of the Party. By the time the Smith Act was passed, whatever threat had once existed of violent overthrow of the government from within the United States had long since disappeared.

In 1951, the Supreme Court reviewed the convictions of twelve members of the central committee of the Communist Party for violating the Smith Act. The evidence at the trial consisted of pamphlets prepared by the defendants advocating the communist political theory that the capitalist government of the United States will someday collapse and that during a transition period, force and violence will be necessary to consolidate the new government. The defendants testified that they personally were not advocating any immediate force or violence and the government introduced no evidence that they had ever suggested that such tactics be used.

With two dissents, the Supreme Court upheld the convictions—without, however, looking at the nature of the evidence. There was no single majority opinion. There were, instead, three different ones. But the gist of the Court's reasoning seemed to be that if the danger be great enough, even in the absence of any immediate threat, the government can put an end to it.

In his dissent, Justice Black noted that the defendants "were not charged with an attempt to overthrow the Government. They were not charged with overt acts of any kind designed to overthrow the Government. They were not even charged with saying anything or writing anything designed to overthrow the Government. The charge was that they agreed to assemble and to talk and publish certain ideas at a later date: The indictment is that they conspired to organize the Communist Party and to use speech or newspapers and other publications in the future to teach and advocate the forcible overthrow of the Government."

To punish people for such activity, Justice Black argued, was the same as prior censorship. And Justice Douglas pointed out that the books the defendants used and referred to in teaching others were not, and could not be, outlawed—in fact, the books could lawfully be used to teach a class what the doctrine of violent overthrow means. The distinction the Court was drawing —a distinction between teaching *about* violent overthrow and actually *advocating* it—was too difficult to draw, he concluded.

Six years later, without actually saying so, the Court did an about-face, and made it virtually impossible to convict anyone under the Smith Act. Fourteen defendants were convicted on charges simliar to those in the 1951 case. Now the Court ruled that the convictions could be upheld only if the defendants advocated action, rather than merely belief in an abstract theory. Moreover, the Court ruled that on examination, the evidence was much too weak to prove that the Communist Party of California (where the cases were tried) was engaged in a conspiracy to overthrow the government. Nor was the evidence against each defendant much stronger. The activity of many of the defendants was no different from that of De Jonge, whose conviction for belonging to a political party the Court had thrown out twenty years earlier. With the Court's ruling by a 6–1 vote that the defendants' convictions had to be reversed, prosecutions under the Smith Act came to an end in the United States.

One important question that remained open was settled four years later, in 1961. That question was whether a person could be guilty of a crime just for belonging to the Communist Party, if it could be shown that the Party really did advocate forcible overthrow of the government. The Court ruled that a member's knowledge of a group's unlawful aims is not enough to establish the member's own personal criminal guilt. Only if the member specifically intends to carry out the unlawful ends of the group may he himself be convicted.

Many civil libertarians believe that the Court did not go far enough in vindicating the First Amendment right to belong to political parties. They argue that proof of knowledge of the group's aims and of the individual's intent to accomplish those aims is difficult to establish. In the heated climate of a "Red scare," when, as once, millions of people were irrationally afraid that a scraggly group of citizens might somehow overthrow the government, a jury could too easily convict on flimsy evidence.

Nevertheless, the Court's decisions in the late 1950s and 1960s have gone a long way to reclaiming for Americans the right to espouse political ideas and to belong to political groups, no matter how noxious a majority of Americans may think those ideas or those groups to be. In such freedom lies considerable security, for the freedom to talk and advocate is also the means by which most people will come to sort out the true and enduring doctrines from those that are plainly silly.

# 5.

# *PUBLIC DISTURBANCES*

The First Amendment provides great leeway for speech and writing about public affairs, even at the risk of considerable damage to the diplomatic interests of the United States or of a change in the fundamental form of government. The First Amendment protects the right to speech and press in the area of public debate because a free people cannot govern themselves if the government blocks the channels of expression.

But what about less cataclysmic evils, where the danger is simply that on the local scene an immediate public disturbance or "breach of the peace" will result from someone's speech: under those circumstances is such a speech also protected by the First Amendment? In this chapter we will consider four such cases.

### THE CASE OF THE FIGHTING WORDS

In the early 1940s a man named Chaplinsky, a Jehovah's Witness (because they are proselytizers, members of this religious sect have figured frequently in First Amendment cases), was distributing some religious literature on the streets near the City Hall of Rochester, New Hampshire, on a busy Saturday afternoon. A crowd began to form, and some of the people complained to the city marshal that Chaplinksy was denouncing all religion as a "racket." The marshal told them that Chaplinksy had the right to speak out but he warned Chaplinsky to watch what he was doing because the crowd was getting "restless." A little while later a disturbance occurred, and the traffic officer on the spot escorted Chaplinsky to the police station—without, however, indicating that he was under arrest.

On the way they ran into the marshal, who had been told that there was a riot at the street corner where Chaplinsky had been orating. The marshal reminded Chaplinsky of his earlier warning. Chaplinsky then turned to the marshal, called him a "damned racketeer" and said he was "a damned fascist and the whole government of Rochester are fascists or agents of fascists." (Chaplinsky's version of the facts differed slightly: he said that he asked the marshal to arrest the people in the crowd who had created the disturbance and the marshal then cursed at him. Only then, Chaplinsky said, did he swear at the marshal. He admitted using the words quoted.)

A New Hampshire ordinance prohibits using offensive or annoying words to anyone in the public streets or calling someone "by any offensive or derisive name." Chaplinsky was arrested for violating this ordinance and convicted in state court. Eventually his appeal came to the U.S. Supreme Court. He said that the ordinance and his conviction invaded his freedom of speech, in violation of the First Amendment.

In a unanimous decision, the Supreme Court disagreed. "There are certain well-defined and narrowly limited classes of speech," Justice Frank Murphy wrote, "the prevention and punishment of which have never been thought to raise any Constitutional problem. These include the lewd and obscene, the profane, the libelous, and the insulting or 'fighting' words—those which by their very utterance inflict injury or tend to incite an immediate breach of the peace." Because the words "damned racketeer" and "damned fascist," spoken to someone's face, are "likely to provoke the average person to retaliation, and thereby cause a breach of the peace," the state law is both constitutional as it is written and as it was applied to Chaplinsky, even though the state courts refused to let him show that he himself had been provoked by the disturbances and the marshal's own words. So "fighting words" lie beyond the protection of the First Amendment.

## THE PUBLIC ANGER CASE

Father Terminiello, an Alabama priest suspended by his local bishop, was invited to address a right-wing group called Christian Veterans of America in an indoor auditorium in Chicago. There was advance publicity for the evening speech and the hall was sold out; many were turned away and because of Terminiello's known extreme right-wing views a hostile crowd of more than 1,500 gathered outside to protest against his appearance. Even as he arrived there was shouting and pushing, and it took a police escort to get Terminiello inside the auditorium. Stones were thrown, pickets tried to block entrance to the building, and loud chants of "fascists" and "Hitlers" could be heard inside. Police were unable to control the mob. Hurled bricks broke twenty-eight windows, and parts of the crowd continued to break into the back door of the auditorium in an attempt to interrupt the program. Police arrested seventeen demonstrators. Inside, Terminiello made a vicious speech, egging on the crowd outside, denouncing various racial and religious groups, political leaders, and others who he claimed were plotting to destroy America. Terminiello's supporters inside the hall were themselves stirred to anger and many shouted such things as "Jews, niggers, and Catholics would have to be gotten rid of."

Terminiello was arrested and tried for the "misdemeanor" (minor crime) of "disorderly conduct"—a violation of a city ordinance. The Chicago law prohibits making "any improper noise, riot, disturbance, breach of the peace." At the trial, the judge instructed the jury that "breach of the peace" includes "misbehavior . . . if it stirs the public to anger, invites dispute, brings about a condition of unrest, or creates a disturbance." Terminiello was found guilty and fined one hundred dollars.

On appeal, the city and state authorities contended that Terminiello's case was no different from Chaplinsky's—that Terminiello used a large number of "fighting words," inciting the crowd to answer and violence, precisely what the city ordinance was intended to punish. But in a 5–4 decision, with bitter dissents, Justice Douglas for the bare Court majority ruled that the judge's instructions, as an interpretation of the city ordinance, were unconstitutional. Wrote Douglas:

> A function of free speech under our system of government is to invite dispute. It may indeed best serve its high purpose when it induces a condition of unrest, creates dissatisfaction with conditions as they are, or even stirs people to anger. Speech is often provocative and challenging. It may strike at prejudices and preconceptions and have profound unsettling effects as it presses for acceptance of an idea. That is why freedom of speech, though not absolute . . . is nevertheless protected against censorship or punishment, unless shown likely to produce a clear and present danger of a serious substantive evil that rises far above public inconvenience, annoyance, or unrest.

Justice Robert H. Jackson wrote a long, stinging dissent, accusing the majority of ignoring "society's need for public order" and reminding his colleagues on the Court that the trial court was "not indulging in theory. It was dealing with a riot and with a speech that provoked a hostile mob and incited a friendly one, and threatened violence between the two."

The Court's ruling, he charged, would be a major hindrance to cities in increasing need of coping with riots and ugly political confrontations: "One faction organizes a mass meeting, the other organizes pickets to harass it; each organizes squads to counteract the other pickets; parade is met with counterparade." Jackson saw the kind of mass meeting that Terminiello addressed and the reactions he provoked as exactly the same in spirit that led to Hitler's rise in Germany during the 1930s. How, Jackson asked, can "this present decision, denying state power to punish civilly one who precipitated a public riot involving hundreds of fanatic fighters in a most violent melee" be squared with the Court's unanimous decision in Chaplinsky's case? Chaplinsky's words, addressed to only one man, were mild, Jackson said, in comparison to terms like "slimy scum," "snakes," and worse that "Terminiello hurled at an already inflamed mob of his adversaries."

Jackson agreed that the

fundamental, permanent and overriding policies of police and courts should be to permit and encourage utmost freedom of utterance. It is the legal right of any American citizen to advocate peaceful adoption of fascism or communism, socialism or capitalism. He may go far in expressing sentiments whether pro-Semitic or anti-Semitic, pro-Negro or anti-Negro, pro-Catholic or anti-Catholic. He is legally free to argue for some anti-American system of government. . . . It is our philosophy that the course of government should be controlled by a consensus of the governed [which requires free discussion]. Hence we should tolerate no law or custom of censorship or suppression.

But we must bear in mind also that no serious outbreak of mob violence, race rioting, lynching or public disorder is likely to get going without help of some speech-making to some mass of people. . . . Passion and hatred, which merges the many minds of a crowd into the mindlessness of a mob, almost invariably is supplied by speeches. . . . No mob has ever protected any liberty, even its own, but if not put down it always winds up in an orgy of lawlessness which respects no liberties.

Jackson's conclusion was that in peaceful surroundings, Terminiello's speech would have been legally permissible but "there certainly comes a point beyond which he cannot [provoke] violence without being answerable to society."

The tension between the majority's declaration of a vast realm of freedom for even the most provocative speech and Justice Jackson's carefully reasoned worries about the dangers of unbridled incitement remains with us, and it always will. Less than two years later, in fact, the Supreme Court came out the other way in a situation where the disturbance was far milder than that in Terminiello's case. But it happened on a street corner.

### THE STREET CORNER HARANGUE CASE

Irving Feiner, a college student, stood on a wooden box on a street corner in Syracuse, New York. Using a loudspeaker attached to an automobile, he addressed a gathering crowd. His purpose in being there was to urge people to come to hear a speech that evening by a former government official on the subject of racial discrimination and civil liberties. Originally the speaker had been scheduled to give his address in a public school, but on the very day of the address the public authorities canceled his permit. The group hosting the meeting, the Young Progressives, a liberal (and some thought radical) political group, rescheduled the speech in a downtown hotel. Feiner was publicizing the meeting and its new location.

The audience consisted of about seventy-five persons, both black and white. In 1949 this was cause for comment, even in Syracuse. More to the point, Feiner made a variety of derogatory comments about government officials. For example, he said, according to police testimony: "President Truman is a bum"; "the American Legion is a Nazi Gestapo"; "the Negroes don't have equal rights; they should rise up in arms and fight for their rights." (There was a dispute as to whether he made this last comment; some witnesses swore he said that his listeners "could rise up and fight for their rights by going arm in arm to the Hotel Syracuse, black and white alike, to hear" the speaker.) Feiner was talking, according to the police, in a "loud, high-pitched voice." In all, he spoke some thirty minutes.

Receiving a telephone complaint, two police officers hurried to the scene. A man in the crowd, which was getting a little excited by Feiner's remarks, told the policemen that if they did not remove Feiner from the box, he would. One of the policemen then approached Feiner and asked him to step down. Feiner ignored him. The policeman waited a couple of minutes, then told him to step down. Again Feiner ignored him, urging his listeners to come to the meeting. Finally, two or three minutes later, the policeman ordered Feiner to stop, reached up to grab him, and told him he was under arrest. Feiner told the crowd that "the law has arrived, and I suppose they will take over now."

At first Feiner was told he had been arrested for "unlawful assembly" but that was soon changed at the police station to "disorderly conduct." A New York State statute, much like the Chicago ordinance in Terminiello's case, declares disorderly conduct to consist in using offensive, abusive or insulting language in public with intent to breach the peace. Or, acting so as to annoy or disturb others. Or, refusing to move on when ordered by the police. Feiner was convicted after trial and sentenced to thirty days in the county penitentiary. The trial judge and the state appeals courts rejected his contention that the police had arrested him to stop him from making remarks with which they disagreed. They said he had been arrested only because a "clear danger of disorder was threatened."

In a 6–3 decision, the Supreme Court agreed that his arrest and conviction were lawful and did not violate his First Amendment rights. "We are well aware," wrote Chief Justice Frederick M. Vinson for the majority, "that the ordinary murmurings and objections of a hostile audience cannot be allowed to silence a speaker, and are also mindful of the possible danger of giving overzealous police officials complete discretion to break up otherwise lawful public meetings. . . . But we are not faced here with such a situation . . . . Here the speaker [passed] the bounds of argument or persuasion and [undertook] incitement to riot."

In dissent, Justice Black said the conviction "makes a mockery of the free speech guarantees" of the First Amendment. "The end result . . . is to approve a simple and readily available technique by which cities and states can . . . subject all speeches, political or otherwise, on streets or elsewhere, to the supervision and censorship of the local police. [This is] a long step toward totalitarian authority." Black noted that it was "farfetched" to say that there was any immediate threat of riot or uncontrollable disorder. It is to be expected that people will mutter and push about at a public gathering. But one isolated threat to assault the speaker (the man who uttered it was accompanied by his wife and two small children) does not mean that a major riot will take place. On the contrary, said Black, the policemen's obligation was to protect the *speaker* by asking the crowd to calm down and by arresting the man who made the threats. Instead, without explanation, the police turned to Feiner and told him to stop doing what everyone agreed he was lawfully entitled to do. "I understand that people in authoritarian countries must obey arbitrary orders," Black wrote. "I had hoped that there was no such duty in the United States."

### THE LABOR PICKETING CASE

Political speechmaking is not the only kind of public appearance that can lead to the kinds of disputes we have just examined. One very important part of American life is the right of labor unions to go out on strike and to picket their office or factory or work site to urge others not to step across the picket line. This was not always understood, as the next case shows.

For several weeks after a strike had been called by the

union, workers picketed the plant of the Brown Wood Preserving Company in Tuscaloosa, Alabama. Between six and eight men manned a picket line. One morning when the company hoped to resume operations at the plant, the union president, Byron Thornhill, who also worked at the plant, was in the picket line and approached one of the few non-union workers at the plant, Clarence Simpson. Thornhill told Simpson they were on strike and did not want anybody "to go up there and work." No one else spoke to Simpson, who later testified that he was never threatened in any way. Simpson acceded to Thornhill's wishes: "I then turned and went back to the house, and did not go to work."

For these activities alone, Thornhill was arrested under an Alabama law that made it a crime to loiter or picket near a place of business with intent either to persuade others not to work there, or in any other way to injure the business. Thornhill was the only person charged with violating this law, though the picketing had been going on for weeks. He was convicted and sentenced to pay a fine of $100 or, if he could not pay that sum, to spend seventy-three days in jail.

The Supreme Court reversed Thornhill's conviction, striking down the law as "invalid on its face." What does this mean? Suppose there were a law that said: "No one may give a speech within the city limits on any topic whatsoever." And suppose that a man stood on a street corner, collected a large crowd around him and began to urge them to break every window in city hall, and that pretty soon they began to move toward city hall, at which point the police came along and arrested the speaker. Now no one has any doubts that a law aimed at stopping such a speaker would be constitutional. But in our example that is not what the law said. The law in our example is much too broad because it prevents all kinds of speeches that are obviously protected by the First Amendment.

If the speaker in this situation were convicted of disorderly conduct, what should the Court do? One thing it could do would be to uphold the conviction on the ground that even though the law was too broad, there is nothing unconstitutional about putting a man in jail for inciting others to break the windows in city hall. But this is not in fact what the Court would do. It would not examine the particular conduct of the convicted person when it came across a law that was too broad. Instead it would strike the law down "on its face"—that is, just by looking at it. Why? Because if the First Amendment is to protect us, laws that interfere with our right to speak must be phrased in as narrow a manner as possible. Otherwise, people who have every right to speak will be afraid that they might be prosecuted. Such fears, which are only natural when there is a broad law, would inhibit many people from speaking or publishing. Since the purpose of the First Amendment is to free us to speak and publish, broad laws that will inhibit the public cannot be upheld. If the legislature wants to outlaw speeches urging others to break windows, it will have to write a narrow law condemning speech intended to lead to a breach of the peace.

So in Thornhill's case, the Court concluded that the law was much too broad. The Court declared, in an opinion by Justice Frank Murphy, that Alabama could not save its law by showing that there might be circumstances under which it would not violate someone's First Amendment rights (for example, if used against someone standing in the doorway of a store and physically preventing those who wanted to from entering). The Alabama statute "sweeps" up all sorts of activities, Justice Murphy said, "that in ordinary circumstances constitute an exercise of freedom of speech or of the press." In an earlier case, Alabama had even used the law "to prohibit a single individual from walking slowly and peacefully back and forth on the public sidewalk in front of the premises of an employer, without speaking to anyone, carrying a sign . . . on a staff above his head stating only the fact that the employer did not employ union men affiliated with the American Federation of Labor." The Alabama law was so broadly phrased that it encompassed "every practical method whereby the facts of a labor dispute may be publicized in the vicinity of the place of business of an employer."

But is picketing about a "private" labor dispute the kind of subject matter that the guarantees of free speech and press were designed to cover? Certainly, said Justice Murphy: "Free discussion concerning the conditions in industry and the causes of labor disputes appears to us indispensable to the effective and intelligent use of the processes of popular government to shape the destiny of modern industrial society." It may be that the picketing will persuade some people to act against the interests of the business being picketed. But that is what free speech is for: "Every expression of opinion on matters that are important has the potentiality of inducing action in the interests of one rather than another group in society. But the group in power at any moment may not . . . [penalize] peaceful and truthful discussion of matters of public interest merely . . . [because] others may thereby be persuaded to take action inconsistent with its interests." The Court noted specifically that it was not talking about a law that narrowly defines its terms in order to outlaw real breaches of the peace. But the broad Alabama statute was not narrow, and the Court declared it void and unenforceable.

### THE COURTHOUSE DEMONSTRATION CASE

Just before Christmas in 1961, twenty-three students from Southern University, a black college in Baton Rouge, Louisiana, were arrested for picketing downtown stores that segregated their lunch counters. The picketing was part of a general protest movement over racial segregation. The Reverend B. Elton Cox, a field secretary of the Congress of Racial Equality, acted as an adviser to the protest movement.

That evening Cox spoke to a mass meeting at the college. The students resolved to demonstrate the next day directly in front of the courthouse where their fellow students were jailed. The following morning two thousand students walked the five miles from their campus to the courthouse. The student body president was arrested as the march began and charged with violating an anti-noise law because she was in a car equipped with a loudspeaker. Cox took over as leader of the march in order to "keep things orderly."

Two and one-half blocks from the courthouse, Cox lined the students up, cautioning them to stay on one side of the sidewalk as they prepared to march to the courthouse. At that point, two police officers arrived and asked Cox what the students intended to do. Cox told them that they planned to protest the "illegal arrest of some of their people who were being held in jail" and that they would march by the courthouse, say prayers, sing hymns, and stay peaceful. The policemen told Cox to disband the group, but Cox refused. While the policemen went off to radio their superiors, the group began to walk to the courthouse.

Just opposite the courthouse, Cox was stopped by one of the original policemen and another, who took him over to the Baton Rouge police chief. Cox told him that the demonstration would include the "Star-Spangled Banner" and a "freedom song," the Lord's Prayer, the Pledge of Allegiance, and a short speech. The police chief, because he could see that he could not stop the huge crowd, told Cox to "confine the demonstration to the west side of the street." The police chief later denied that he was thereby giving permission for the protest, but Cox and some witnesses said that that was the deal.

Cox led the students across the street from the courthouse steps. They lined up five feet deep down almost the entire length of the block, but did not block traffic in the street. It was almost noon. A group of some 100 to 300 whites in the streets stopped to watch. There were seventy-five to eighty policemen, as well as fire trucks, stationed all around. It was raining during the entire demonstration.

As it began, several students took pickets signs from underneath their coats, saying such things as "Don't buy discrimination for Christmas." The singing and prayers began. The twenty-three students in jail heard the singing and began to sing themselves. The crowd heard this and cheered.

Cox then gave his speech. He protested the illegal arrest but said that they ought all remain peaceful. A witness later testified that Cox said no one was going to commit violence and that if anyone spit on them they would not spit back on the person who did it. Then Cox said: "All right. It's lunch time. Let's go eat. There are twelve stores we are protesting. A number of these stores have twenty counters; they accept your money from nineteen. They won't accept it from the twentieth [the lunch] counter. This is an action of racial discrimination." Some witnesses said there was grumbling and muttering by some of the white onlookers.

At that point the city sheriff took up a microphone and addressed the students. He told them that "up until now" the demonstration had been peaceful but that what Cox was urging was "a direct violation of the law, a disturbance of the peace, and it has to be broken up immediately."

Cox did not move to disband the group. Some of the sheriff's deputies went into the street and began to push the students away. Within a couple of minutes, a policeman fired a tear gas shell into the crowd, which quickly dispersed as more tear gas was fired at them. Cox tried to calm the students down and stayed until they all left. No one was arrested except one young white man, who was not part of the students' demonstration.

The following day, however, the police arrested Cox and charged him with four violations of law, including breach of the peace, obstructing public passages, and picketing before a courthouse. He was convicted on the charges just named and sentenced to twenty-one months in jail and $5,700 in fines.

His appeal came before the Supreme Court more than three years later, in 1965. By a 6–3 vote, the Court upheld Cox's position and dismissed all the charges. Once again, the Court found that the state law was much too broad to survive a legal attack on First Amendment grounds. Under the state law, a person could be convicted of breach of the peace "merely for peacefully expressing unpopular views." But doing so is protected by the First Amendment, so the breach of peace conviction had to be reversed.

The law against obstructing public passages was aimed at groups of people who intend to disrupt streets and traffic. Cox's conviction under this law meant that the state courts "construed" (interpreted) the law to apply to situations where the group had no such purpose, even though it was clear that the far sidewalk across from the court was in fact obstructed. Nevertheless, such a law is not invalid on its face. A city has the right to keep order on its public streets and sidewalks. (In Chapter 8 we will examine problems with laws designed to do so.) The problem was that this law set forth no standards for public officials to follow in determining whether to allow parades or marches. The law on its face says there are to be no parades or demonstrations, but the facts showed that the authorities had permitted many in the past. A law giving such "uncontrolled discretion" to public officials amounts to a prior restraint, for they can pick and choose whomever they want to talk and whatever they want to be heard and deny permission to the rest.

One charge—the most serious one—remained. That was a violation of a law against picketing near a courthouse. It carried a maximum fine of $5,000 and one year in jail. The Court refused to declare the law unconstitutional on its face because the statute had been carefully drafted to deal with a specific harm the Court thought it proper to legislate against—namely, public gatherings that intimidated or appeared to intimidate judges from carrying out their duties under law. But the Court nevertheless ruled that it could not be used as the basis of a conviction in Cox's case. Why?

The result did not depend on the First Amendment but instead on the "Due Process Clause" of the Fourteenth Amendment. Under that clause, a person may not be held guilty of a crime if laws are too vague to know what they mean or if he is tricked into violating the laws. The courthouse picketing law did not say how close a demonstration could come to a courthouse and still be lawful; it simply said no one could picket "near" a courthouse. This is a vague term, and when the police said that as long as Cox kept his group across the street they could continue with their protest, the police were telling him that that was far enough away. Otherwise they would in effect be tricking him into violating the law, for at no time did they warn him that the protest violated the courthouse picketing law. If it did, the police should have arrested him as the protest got under way, not a day after it was all over. So the Court reversed his conviction on all counts, and Cox went free.

# 6.

## *NON-VERBAL SPEECH*

This chapter title may look like a contradiction in terms. What kind of "speech" can be non-verbal? Speech deals with words. Is there any kind of speech beyond the oral speech of the street corner orator (or television and radio broadcasters) or the written words published by newspapers, magazines, or in books?

The answer must surely be that there is—and a very important kind, at that. Watch closely the next time someone talks to you. Don't look at the face but at the hands and arms and shoulders. People frequently gesticulate: fingers waggling, arms waving, shoulders shrugging. These gestures are meaningful: body language can communicate thoughts and feelings. So too can art: pictures, sculpture, music. Would anyone ever stoop to censoring music? The sad answer is that in many nations today certain kinds of music cannot be played because the rulers fear for the "security" of the nation. Until recently, the greatest symphonies of the western world were frowned on in China. And in July 1979 *all* music was banned from radio and television by the Islamic government of Iran.

Is non-verbal speech protected by the First Amendment? The answer is easy for many types of expression, like painting. It is protected. But difficult questions can arise when the "speaker" claims that not merely his speech but his acts amount to communication. We will look at three cases to see how the Court has dealt with this problem.

## THE DRAFT-CARD BURNING CASE

On March 31, 1966, with anti-war fever beginning to spread across college campuses and other places throughout the United States, David Paul O'Brien and three friends burned their Selective Service registration certificates (draft cards) on the steps of the South Boston Courthouse. Federal law then required men between the ages of eighteen and thirty-five to carry these cards with them. Deliberately destroying a draft card carried criminal penalties.

Outside the courthouse there was a large crowd that included FBI agents. Immediately after the burning, several members of the crowd began to attack O'Brien and his companions. An FBI agent whisked them inside to safety. O'Brien told the FBI agents that he knew he was violating the federal statute but that he did so out of personal conscience and in the hopes that it would influence others to consider and adopt his anti-war position.

At his trial and on appeal, O'Brien admitted what he had done but asserted that it was unconstitutional to outlaw draft-card burning. Setting his card in flames was a way of calling attention to his beliefs and dramatizing opposition to the Vietnam war. In short, he claimed his act was "symbolic speech." He argued that "communication of ideas by conduct" is protected by the First Amendment and that his conduct fell within his definition of symbolic speech because he burned his card in "demonstration against the war and against the draft."

The Supreme Court disagreed. There is nothing about the law on its face that makes it unconstitutional, Chief Justice Warren wrote in his majority opinion. "A law prohibiting destruction of Selective Service certificates no more abridges free speech on its face than a motor vehicle law prohibiting the destruction of drivers' licenses, or a tax law prohibiting the destruction of books and records."

Even as applied to O'Brien, the law is not unconstitutional. Said the Chief Justice: "We cannot accept the view that an apparently limitless variety of conduct can be labeled 'speech' whenever the person engaging in the conduct intends thereby to express an idea." The constitutional test of a law prohibiting conduct that someone claims is symbolic speech is this:

1. Congress must have the constitutional authority to pass the law. In O'Brien's case, Congress had the power to raise and support armies. The draft was a part of the system of calling up soldiers.

2. The law must be aimed at supporting an important governmental interest. Raising an army is certainly such an interest, and the draft card was an important element in the process by which the government undertook to do so.

3. The law must not be related to the suppression of free expression. This law was not aimed at suppressing dissent about American foreign policy. It was aimed at making the Selective Service system efficient. (On the other hand, a law that said no one could ridicule the Army, on the ground that it would be easier to conduct a war without everyone's joking about the Army, would obviously be aimed at suppressing speech and would be unconstitutional.)

4. Any incidental restriction on First Amendment freedoms must be only broad enough to further the interest that caused Congress to legislate in the first place. Again, Congress was not legislating against dissent; it simply wanted draft cards kept whole to make them useful in the draft system. The effect of the law was not to prevent anyone from saying anything he wanted to about the draft, the war, or anything else.

## THE IMPROPER USE OF A FLAG CASE

In May 1970, Harold O. Spence, a college student, hung his personal American flag upside down from a window in his apartment building in Seattle, Washington. Attached to the front and back was the familiar peace symbol (a "trident" in a circle) made out of black tape. Although he lived above the ground floor, the flag was clearly visible to pedestrians; it measured three by five feet and the peace symbol was half as large as the flag.

Three policemen, seeing the flag, came into the building. Spence was standing at the main door. He said to them: "I suppose you are here about the flag. I didn't know there was anything wrong with it. I will take it down." Spence let the policemen enter his apartment, where they not only confiscated the flag but arrested him. The charge was "improper use" of the flag. Under Washington State law, it was unlawful to display an American flag that had any "word, figure, mark, picture, design, drawing, or advertisement" on it. The law was not confined to regular flags made of cloth. It covered any copy or drawing of a flag regardless of how it was made or on what it was placed.

At his trial, Spence said he had displayed the flag to protest the American invasion of Cambodia and the shooting of students at Kent State University. Both of these events had occurred a few days before he put the flag out the window. He wanted to associate the flag with peace rather than war, he said, adding: "I felt there had been so much killing and that this was not what America stood for. I felt that the flag stood for America and I wanted people to know that I thought America stood for peace." He was convicted by the jury after the trial judge instructed them, in a manner reminiscent of Zenger's case, that he was guilty if it was proved that he had displayed the flag with the peace symbol on it—an act which Spence freely admitted. He was given a ten-day suspended jail sentence and a $75 fine. The Washington Supreme Court upheld his conviction.

On appeal to the U.S. Supreme Court, Spence won his case. The Court began by noting that Spence's use of the flag was entirely peaceful, not intended to incite violence or a breach of the peace nor had it done so. It was his own flag and it was displayed on private property. He trespassed nowhere and engaged in no disorderly conduct.

What Spence did do, the Court agreed, was to communicate through the use of symbols. Moreover, he chose these particular symbols at a time when "it would have been difficult for the majority of citizens to miss the drift of [his] point." What the case amounted to, then, was a "prosecution for the expression of an idea through activity."

The State argued that it "has an interest in preserving the national flag as an unalloyed symbol of our country." Why should it have such an interest? There are a couple of possible reasons. It might want to prevent someone from trying to associate the flag with a particular idea or product and thus lead others to believe the idea or product was endorsed by the government. Or it might be desirous of preserving one symbol as a universal expression of the American ideal, whatever that may be.

The Supreme Court did not decide whether such an interest by the State of Washington was valid. Even assuming that it is, the Court ruled, the law is still unconstitutional as it was applied to Spence, for no conceivable interest of the state was impaired by what he did.

### THE BLACK ARMBAND CASE

At a meeting in a private home in Des Moines, Iowa, in December 1965, a group of adults and students decided to publicize their opposition to the growing war in Vietnam. One member of the group was a Methodist minister working for the American Friends Service Committee. He had four children in the Des Moines public schools; his oldest, John Tinker, was then fifteen and in the eleventh grade. The mother of John's classmate, Christopher Eckhardt, was also at the meeting; she was an official in the Women's International League for Peace and Freedom. The group concluded that their protest should take the form of wearing black cloth bands on their arms during the holiday

season and to fast on two days. This was not the first time they
had engaged in a protest movement of this sort in this way, and
they resolved it was time to do so again.

Principals at the Des Moines schools got wind of the plan,
however, and adopted a rule against wearing armbands. Any
student seen wearing one to school would be asked to remove it.
If the student refused, he or she would be suspended. Readmit-
tance to school depended on a change of heart about wearing
the armband.

When John Tinker, his younger sister Mary Beth, then in
the eighth grade, and Christopher Eckhardt all came to school
wearing black armbands, they were sent home and suspended.
They did not return until after New Year's Day, the end of the
period the group had set as the time for wearing the protest badge.

The fathers of the students sued the school officials to
enjoin them from punishing their children. The lower federal
courts agreed with the school authorities that it was proper for
schools to set rules for discipline and that a rule prohibiting
the wearing of black armbands was reasonable, since it helped
prevent disturbances in the schools.

In a 7–2 decision, the Supreme Court reversed the lower
courts and held that wearing a black armband is a constitutionally
protected form of "speech." In his opinion for the Court, Justice
Abe Fortas noted that there was no evidence of any effort by
the students wearing armbands—only seven out of 18,000 students did so—to disrupt the schools or the classrooms. A few
non-wearers made hostile remarks to those who bore the bands,
but there was no threat or act of violence anywhere on the
school grounds. The fear of the school authorities that there
might be disturbances was not enough to justify the ban, Fortas
declared:

> In our system, [a general fear of disturbance] is not
> enough to overcome the right to freedom of expression.
> Any departure from absolute regimentation may cause
> trouble. Any variation from the majority's opinion may

inspire fear. Any word spoken, in class, in the lunch-
room, or on the campus, that deviates from the views
of another person may start an argument or cause a
disturbance. But our Constitution says we must take
this risk.

What the school authorities really wanted, Fortas asserted,
was "to avoid the controversy which might result from the expression, even by the silent symbol of armbands, of opposition to
this Nation's part in the conflagration in Vietnam." Moreover,
it was significant that the school officials did not prohibit wearing other symbols with political and controversial overtones.
For example, some students wore political campaign buttons and
some even wore the Iron Cross, a Nazi symbol from the 1930s
and 1940s. But school officials banned only the black armbands.
"Clearly," said Fortas, "the prohibition of expression of one particular opinion, at least without evidence that it is necessary
to avoid [real] interference with schoolwork or discipline, is
not constitutionally permissible."

To those who said that the armbands could be suppressed
because there were plenty of other places to wear them, Justice
Fortas answered:

Freedom of expression would not truly exist if the
right could be exercised only in an area that a be-
nevolent government has provided as a safe haven for
crackpots. . . . [The First Amendment] means what
it says. . . . We do not confine the permissible exercise of First Amendment rights to a telephone booth
or the four corners of a pamphlet, or to supervised and
ordained discussion in a school classroom.

The Court was careful to note, however, that its upholding
the right to wear armbands does not mean that officials are
powerless to make regulations for the discipline of schools. If
there had been evidence that a major confrontation might occur

that would have interrupted classwork, the school could have banned the bands. Also, the armband case does not relate to the regulation of types of clothing, hair style, or behavior. Although the majority opinion did not say so, it clearly implied that schools may constitutionally adopt rules relating to these areas.

# 7.

## THE FREEDOM
## NOT TO SPEAK

The First Amendment, as we have seen by now, has a very wide sweep. It protects all sorts of speaking and writing concerned with public affairs, even at the risk of disturbing or angering the listeners or the government. Moreover, it is not limited to words: it covers at least limited actions, where those can be described as basically conveying a message symbolically. But is the First Amendment even broader? Does it give people the right *not* to speak—to refrain from expressing opinions or beliefs that others wish they would utter? As the following two cases show, the Constitution is indeed that broad.

### THE FLAG SALUTE CASE

In 1941 the State of West Virginia passed a law requiring all schools—private, parochial, and public—to give instruction in history, civics, and the federal and state constitutions. The law was enacted "for the purpose of teaching, fostering and perpetuating the ideals, principles and spirit of Americanism, and increasing the knowledge of the organization and machinery of the government." Under this law, the Board of Education was empowered to detail the content of these courses. In early 1942, the Board ordered, as part of the curriculum that it devised, that a salute to the flag become "a regular part of the program of activities in the public schools." Every student and teacher was required to salute the flag. Anyone refusing to do so, the Board decreed, could be punished for insubordination, which meant expulsion. As long as a child remained expelled from school, his absence could be treated as unlawful and he could be prosecuted as a delinquent and his parents could be fined and jailed.

A group of Jehovah's Witnesses filed suit in federal court to enjoin the enforcement of these rules and to forestall the consequences just outlined for failing to salute the flag. Their objection is based on their religious belief that the law of God, as written in the Book of Exodus, is binding on them. The command of the Bible (Exodus, ch. 20, v. 4–5) is as follows: "Thou shalt not make unto thee any graven image, or any likeness of anything that is in heaven above, or that is in the earth beneath, or that is in the water under the earth; thou shalt not bow down thyself to them nor serve them." Interpreting this command literally, the Witnesses consider the flag an "image" and refuse to salute it.

Instead, they offered to give the following pledge "periodically and publicly": "I respect the flag of the United States and acknowledge it as a symbol of freedom and justice to all. I pledge allegiance and obedience to all the laws of the United States that are consistent with God's laws, as set forth in the Bible." The Board of Education refused to accept this pledge as a substitute for a salute to the flag and the standard Pledge of Allegiance. When children of Jehovah's Witnesses refused to salute and recite the Pledge, they were expelled. Officials even threatened to send some to reformatories.

The lower court ruled that the Board's flag salute requirement violated various provisions of the Constitution, and it enjoined the Board from enforcing the law against any Jehovah's Witness. The State of West Virginia appealed to the Supreme Court, and there, in a 6–3 decision, lost its case for good.

No one questioned the right of a state to require instruction in history and government, Justice Jackson began the majority opinion. In this case, however, "we are dealing with a compulsion of students to declare a belief." Their unwillingness to do so didn't interfere with the rights of others to do so voluntarily, nor did anyone doubt that the Witnesses' "behavior is peaceable and orderly."

The past decisions of the Supreme Court relating to the First Amendment—the "precedents" on the subject—make it very clear that "censorship or suppression of expression of opinion is tolerated by our Constitution only when the expression presents a clear and present danger of action of a kind the State is empowered to prevent and punish." This case presented the reverse: an involuntary expression of opinion. That can only be justified by pointing to "even more immediate and urgent grounds" than that required to silence someone. But West Virginia had no such grounds. What "clear and present danger" would be presented if someone sat still during a flag ceremony? To order students to salute, the Court would have to conclude that "a Bill of Rights which guards the individual's right to speak his own mind left it open to public authorities to compel him to utter what is not in his mind." This conclusion the Court could not accept.

The argument favoring compulsory flag salute rested on one fundamental proposition: that "national unity is the basis of national security" and that the state has the power to seek national unity through various means, including the patriotic act of saluting the flag. But, said Justice Jackson, such molding of opinion is exactly what the First Amendment was designed to avoid. "Those who begin coercive elimination of dissent soon find themselves exterminating dissenters. To believe that patriotism will not flourish if patriotic ceremonies are voluntary and spontaneous instead of a compulsory routine is to make an unflattering estimate of the appeal of our institutions to free minds." If a person were to be free to differ with his fellows only in ways that didn't matter, "that would be a mere shadow of freedom,"

Justice Jackson said, adding one of the most quoted concise definitions of freedom ever to come from the Supreme Court:

> If there is any fixed star in our constitutional constellation, it is that no official, high or petty, can prescribe what shall be orthodox in politics, nationalism, religion, or other matters of opinion or force citizens to confess by word or act their faith therein.

### THE LOYALTY OATH CASE

One of the many types of laws enacted during the late 1940s and 1950s, in the midst of the scare over Communist "infiltration" of the government, was that which required all sorts of public employees to take "loyalty oaths." The oath is an ancient device, used by kings and others to bind subjects to them. Under the Constitution, the President of the United States is required to take an oath of office, as are members of Congress, justices of the Supreme Court and other judges, and all members of the executive branch of the federal government.

There can be no quarrel with this requirement that public officials solemnly pledge to support the Constitution and laws and be loyal to the nation whose government they serve. But, as we have just seen, there can be great difficulties if ordinary citizens are forced to declare a set of beliefs. One of the reasons that the early colonists came to the United States was to avoid religious oaths they were required to swear in England.

Many types of government jobs are not official in the usual sense. Public school teachers, for example, work for governments, since city and state governments run elementary and secondary schools and universities—but teachers are not officials in the sense that a President or a senator or a justice is. Moreover, the loyalty oaths in many states were not simply pledges of allegiance. They called on public employees to swear that they were not members of certain political organizations, such as the Communist Party.

Without taking the oath, the employee could not take the job. Most of these oaths were not narrowly drawn, and they seemed to be designed to prevent all sorts of people with unconventional political beliefs from taking state and local jobs. Sometimes even people of perfectly ordinary political beliefs, who were not members of the Communist Party or anything like it, refused to take the oath as a matter of conscience, because it was not clear what the oath meant. One such case arose in Arizona during the 1960s.

The Arizona oath is a familiar one. It required the prospective employee to

> solemnly swear (or affirm) that I will support the Constitution of the United States and the Constitution and laws of the state of Arizona; that I will bear true faith and allegiance to the same, and defend them against all enemies whatever, and that I will faithfully and impartially discharge the duties of the office, according to the best of my ability, so help me God (or so I do affirm).

On its face, the oath presents no problems: it is almost word-for-word the same as that taken by federal officials. But the Arizona legislature created a problem. It passed a law saying that if anyone took the oath who at the time was or later became a member of the Communist Party or "any other organization" having for "one of its purposes" the overthrow of the government, he could be fired and prosecuted for perjury (assuming he knew about the purposes of the organization). In short, the Arizona law converted the oath from one of allegiance to a statement of personal political principles.

Barbara Elfbrandt was a teacher and a Quaker. Her conscience forbade her to take the oath because she didn't know what it meant or how far it extended. She couldn't get a hearing from any state official or agency to clarify its meaning. So she sued to prevent state authorities from forcing her to take the oath. The case came before the Supreme Court in 1966 and, writing for a bare 5–4 majority, Justice Douglas concluded that the law interpreting the oath was too vague to be upheld.

The problem was that a person can be a member of a group and not share all of its purposes. For example, many international scientific organizations have members from communist countries. If such an organization came to be dominated by foreigners, one of its purposes might be to overthrow the government in the United States, even if that were not the main purpose. Under the Arizona law, a person belonging to such an organization could be fired and prosecuted even though she didn't subscribe to the group's unlawful purpose. But this imposes too much of a burden: "Public employees of character and integrity may well forgo their calling rather than risk prosecution for perjury or compromise their commitment to intellectual and political freedom."

So the Supreme Court ruled the Arizona law unconstitutional.

# 8.

## *WHERE AND HOW MAY SPEAKING AND PUBLISHING BE DONE?*

To say that we are free to say or publish *whatever* we please does not mean that we may say it *whenever* or *wherever* we please. The First Amendment prohibits government from interfering with the *content* of our spoken and printed thoughts, but it could hardly forbid government to regulate the *manner* in which our ideas are transmitted to others. Otherwise, a person could stand out in the middle of a street and stop traffic to tell passing motorists his thoughts. Or he could break into a private home and deliver a speech over a loudspeaker to an unwilling party gathered in the living room. Demonstrators could claim the right to march anywhere they wanted anytime they liked for as long as they could hold out from hunger and fatigue. Obviously, government must be able to protect a community from invasions of privacy and from interference with the normal use of the city streets.

But the power to regulate is nevertheless a dangerous thing. The line between the manner of expression and the content of expression, or the ability to speak out, is often difficult to draw. Sometimes the regulation, while it may appear fair and reasonable, may nevertheless intrude too deeply on our First Amendment rights. Let's turn to three areas where special problems recur: door-to-door solicitation, the use of sound trucks in public places, and regulation of littering.

## THE DOOR-TO-DOOR SOLICITOR CASES

Most people are familiar with door-to-door salesmen. Selling brushes, cosmetics, magazines, or soliciting for a charity, such people can provide a useful service or be an extreme annoyance. Many people find especially irritating those who, uninvited, ring doorbells to pass out political pamphlets or religious tracts. Many cities have sought to restrict the ability of solicitors to go from door to door.

One way to regulate solicitors is to set up a licensing scheme. This is what the town of Irvington, New Jersey, did in the late 1930s. It passed an ordinance prohibiting anyone from soliciting, distributing circulars, or going from house to house "without first having reported to and received a written permit from the Chief of Police." The permit would list the specific number of hours or days it was good for, and the applicant had to fill out a long form listing such things as physical characteristics, arrest record, employment history, and description of what he intended to go house to house for. The applicant had to be fingerprinted. The police chief was entitled to refuse a permit to anyone "not of good character" or where it appeared that the solicitation was for some fraudulent purpose. The solicitor was required to refrain from "importuning" or "annoying" the town's inhabitants.

A Jehovah's Witness was arrested for canvassing from house to house without a permit. She would call on people at all times of the day and night, leave some booklets, and ask for a contribution to enable more booklets to be printed in order to be given out to others. She was convicted and the state courts denied that any First Amendment right had been abridged.

But the Supreme Court thought otherwise. Justice Owen Roberts, for an 8–1 Court majority, noted that the licensing scheme was not limited simply to those interested in making a profit or to ordinary peddlers. Nor was it enacted to prohibit trespassing. It was, rather, quite broad, since it applied equally to anyone who wished to present his or her views on political, social, or economic questions. The police chief was given the power to censor "what literature may be distributed from house to house and who may distribute it." The effect of the permit system, which was a burden to comply with, was to reduce the freedom of people to disseminate opinion through one of the most effective ways known: namely, by bringing literature right to the front door of people's homes. In short, the system amounted to a prior restraint. If the town wished to combat fraud or trespass, it certainly could do so by punishing the person who actually committed fraud or trespass. Although the town could regulate the hours during which people could make such door-to-door visits, it could not constitutionally give the police chief discretion to decide who should receive a permit to go from house to house.

The City of Struthers, Ohio, passed a different kind of ordinance. It gave its public officials no discretion at all; instead, it simply banned all house-to-house visits. Its ordinance read: "It is unlawful for any person distributing handbills, circulars, or other advertisements to ring the door bell, sound the door knockers, or otherwise summon the inmate or inmates of any residence to the door for the purpose of receiving such handbills, circulars or other advertisements."

In support of its ordinance, the city pointed out that most of its residents were engaged in the iron and steel industry and worked on "swing shifts," meaning that many worked nights and slept days. "Although they call at high noon," door-to-door solicitors might seriously interfere with the sleep of many people. Moreover, posing as a salesman or other solicitor is a common way for burglars to learn whether someone is home or a house is empty. So for both reasons, the city argued that it could constitutionally regulate solicitation by banning it altogether.

The Supreme Court disagreed. Pointing to a variety of groups that distribute literature, political pamphlets, and labor and business information and to the technique of political campaigning and seeking signatures for petitions, Justice Black declared that "freedom to distribute information to every citizen wherever he desires to receive it is so clearly vital to the preservation of a free society that (aside from reasonable regulations dealing with the time and manner of distribution) it must be fully preserved. The dangers of distribution can so easily be controlled by traditional legal methods, leaving to each householder the full right to decide whether he will receive strangers as visitors, that stringent prohibition can serve no purpose but . . . the naked restriction of ideas."

In 1951 the Court dealt with an ordinance that followed through on Justice Black's suggestion that the householders themselves could decide not to allow strangers to come to their homes uninvited. The City of Alexandria, Louisiana, outlawed house-to-house selling or distributing unless the "solicitors, peddlers, hawkers, itinerant merchants or transient vendors of merchandise" first had received permission by the owner or occupant. Jack Breard was arrested and convicted for going door to door, without prior consent of each owner, to sell nationally circulated magazines. It was not practical for him to obtain prior consent because he was in charge of a crew of salesmen who stayed only a few days in each town and tried to drum up as many subscriptions as they could while they were there. To have spent time telephoning or writing in advance would have been impractical and much more costly. Breard insisted he had a right to go door to door.

The Supreme Court disagreed. A city can require that peddlers first obtain consent of homeowners or occupants, Justice Stanley Reed said for the 6 to 3 majority, because it is only regulating the manner in which solicitors may work. Such a regulation does not prevent anyone from getting a subscription to a magazine, nor does it prevent anyone from offering one by coming to the door if invited. The ordinance applies equally to the seller of a magazine or of pots and pans; it was not aimed simply at those who deal in printed journals and magazines.

Justice Black dissented. He said homeowners could post a sign saying that they did not want solicitors calling on them but in the absence of such a sign, the First Amendment, he believed, prohibits those "who peacefully go from door to door as agents of the press" from being punished.

## THE NOISE POLLUTION CASES

The First Amendment was written in the days when the only way of talking louder was to shout. At best, an orator could be heard only so many feet in front of him. Today, of course, electronic amplification can carry a voice over great distances and can disturb the relative tranquillity of many public places. To deal with this nuisance, many towns began to adopt ordinances to silence the loudspeakers.

One such town was Lockport, New York, which in the 1940s forbade the use of any electronic amplifier that could broadcast voices onto the public streets or other public places if the broadcast was done for advertising purposes. The ordinance did allow radio broadcasts of news and athletic activities in public places, but only if permission had first been obtained from the chief of police.

Once again, a case testing the legitimacy of such a law came from the activities of a Jehovah's Witness. Unlike some of his co-religionists, who believed that seeking permits to spread the gospel was against God's law, this particular minister, Samuel Saia, went to the police for a permit to operate a loudspeaker mounted on top of his car. He wanted to broadcast lectures on religious topics in a public park at fixed times on certain Sundays. He was given a permit for a limited time. After the permit expired he went back to the police for another one, but this time the police refused to give him one on the ground that complaints had been made about the noise. Saia went back to the park anyway and broadcast lectures on four separate occasions. He was arrested, convicted, and sentenced to fines and jail. The state courts ruled that the ordinance was constitutional, and once again a Jehovah's Witness took his case to the U.S. Supreme Court where, in 1948 in a close 5–4 decision, he prevailed and the ordinance was struck down.

Justice Douglas said that the law was invalid on its face. As in a series of earlier cases involving door-to-door solicitation and public meetings, the Lockport law gave too much discretion to local officials to censor thoughts they didn't want others to hear. "There are no standards prescribed for the exercise of [the police chief's] discretion," Justice Douglas wrote. "The statute is not narrowly drawn to regulate the hours or places of use of loudspeakers, or the volume of sound (the decibels) to which they must be adjusted."

But the loudspeaker does make noise. Cannot a city limit its uses so as to let people enjoy a public park in peace and quiet? Yes, said Justice Douglas: "Noise can be regulated by regulating decibels. The hours and place of public discussion can be controlled." But that is not what was done in Lockport. There the police chief had no rules to guide him. "In this case," Justice Douglas noted, "a permit is denied because some persons were said to have found the sound annoying. In the next one a permit may be denied because some people find the ideas annoying. Annoyance at ideas can be cloaked in annoyance at sound."

In his majority opinion, Justice Douglas said something else as well. He asserted that while the First Amendment allows a city to regulate the hours and place and noise level of loudspeaker use, it does not permit local government to ban loudspeakers altogether, because "loudspeakers are today indispensable instruments of effective public speech." In other words, the First Amendment protects not merely a person's right to say what he pleases; it also protects his right to spread his ideas with the aid of modern inventions. "To allow the police to bar the use of loudspeakers because their use can be abused is like barring radio receivers because they too make a noise," he said.

But Justice Douglas's contention that the loudspeaker as such is protected by the First Amendment turned out to be wrong. The very next year the Supreme Court ruled that a city could ban outright the use of loudspeakers in public places.

The case came from Trenton, New Jersey, which had a law that read as follows: "It shall be unlawful . . . to use or operate for advertising purposes, or for any other purpose whatsoever, on the public streets, alleys or thoroughfares in the City of Trenton, any device known as a sound truck, loud speaker or sound amplifier, or radio or phonograph with a loud speaker or sound amplifier."

A man named Kovacs was arrested and convicted for play-ing music and broadcasting a speech from a sound truck near the city municipal building. Although it was not clear exactly what the purpose of his broadcast was, it appeared that he was using his sound truck "to comment on a labor dispute," surely a matter of public concern. If he had simply been speaking nor-mally on the street corner, he would have been entitled to do so without question. Kovacs objected that an absolute prohibition against using his sound equipment violated his rights as well. The New Jersey Supreme Court said, however, that the law was not vague because it applied only to vehicles with sound equip-ment and prohibited them only on public streets. Use of sound equipment in public parks or other public places was not for-bidden. Moreover, the right to use sound equipment in these places was not subject to the prior approval of the police chief or any other public official.

The Supreme Court agreed. In a 6–3 decision it ruled that the Trenton law was valid and sustained Kovacs' conviction. But wasn't this like the case of the law in Struthers, Ohio, which banned all door-to-door solicitations? The Court struck down that law, after all. Why not, then, ban this law, for it also con-tains an absolute ban? The difference, Justice Reed said, was that homeowners could protect themselves against unwanted intrusions by posting a sign telling solicitors to stay away. But in that case the Court never said "that the visitor could insert a foot in the door and insist on a hearing." The problem with sound trucks is that it is impossible to avoid them: "The unwill-ing listener is not like the passersby who may be offered a pamphlet in the street but cannot be made to take it. In his home or on the street he is practically helpless to escape this interference with his privacy by loud speakers" unless the city steps in and outlaws it.

In his dissent, Justice Black argued that "the basic premise of the First Amendment is that all present instruments of com-munication, as well as others that inventive genius may bring into being, shall be free from governmental censorship or pro-hibition. . . . Laws like this Trenton ordinance can give an overpowering influence to views of owners of legally favored instruments of communication." Black said that it was the *absolute* ban that in his judgment was what made the law unconstitutional. A city could ban the use of amplifiers on busy streets in the business area, he said, and it could also set a maximum volume level and limit the hours during which sound trucks could operate. But the majority disagreed and so the law stands.

## THE LITTERING CASES

Still another class of cases has arisen concerning many of these same problems. These are the cases that deal with laws designed to control litter on public streets. A familiar sight in every sizable city and in many smaller towns today is the street corner hawker who passes out handbills and other circulars. The rules that developed to control their activity parallel those concerned with door-to-door solicitation and use of the public streets.

In 1938, in one of its earliest rulings on the subject of regulating the time and place of speech, in fact, the Supreme Court struck down an ordinance of Griffin, Georgia. The city required anyone who wanted to distribute literature of any sort on the city streets to get written permission in advance from the city manager. By now, the reason for throwing out this law should be clear. It is a prior restraint on exercise of the right to speak and publish. The City of Griffin argued that the law was designed as a health measure to prevent the streets from being drenched in paper litter. The City also argued that handbills and circulars have nothing to do with newspapers and magazines, for which the First Amendment was intended. The Supreme Court's opinion invalidating the law was unanimous. "The liberty of the press," Chief Justice Hughes declared, "is not confined to newspapers and periodicals. It necessarily embraces pamphlets and leaflets." The importance of pamphleteering was well known to the Founding Fathers; indeed, the pamphlets of Thomas Paine and others in the 1770s helped spark the War for

Independence. It did not matter that the City claimed it was not regulating *publication* but only *distribution* of circulars and other material, for without the right to circulate printed material, the right to publish would be of little value.

But suppose that no public official could pick and choose among those who wanted to hand out leaflets. Suppose a city banned such distribution altogether, in the interests of clean streets. Los Angeles had such a law. It forbade handing out any circular, booklet, poster, letter, or other printed material to pedestrians on the streets, on sidewalks, or in parks. It also prohibited putting such material on automobiles. A man was arrested and convicted for handing out notices of a meeting to discuss the war then raging in Spain. In 1939 the Supreme Court heard an appeal in that case and joined it with other similar cases. One came from Milwaukee, where a man distributed a leaflet discussing a labor dispute; another came from Worcester, Massachusetts, where a number of people passed out circulars announcing a protest meeting in connection with problems of state unemployment insurance.

Again, the Court threw out all these laws. The burden on the city of cleaning up the streets is too tiny to offset the great importance in keeping open the channels of communication. That does not mean that cities cannot deal with street littering, the Court said. "There are obvious methods of preventing littering. Amongst these is the punishment of those who actually throw papers on the streets."

## THE CASE OF THE SUBMARINE ADVERTISEMENT

The Court has not always struck down every anti-littering law. One case in particular is worth looking at for the problems it created. A man named F. J. Chrestensen bought an old U.S. Navy submarine, moored it in New York City at a pier in the East River, and charged admission. To advertise his tour, he printed up a handbill telling about the ship and stating the admission fee. As he began distributing these handbills on the streets, he was told by the police that a city ordinance prohibited the circulation of any printed materials dealing with "commercial and business advertising matter." He could distribute handbills having solely to do with "information or a public protest."

So Chrestensen went back to work and prepared a new handbill. On one side was his message about his ship, with the statement about the admission fee removed. This side, he said, was "information." On the other side, he printed a protest against the city docks department for its refusal to cooperate with him. He showed this new double-sided handbill to the police department before he had copies printed up. The police department told him that he could distribute a handbill dealing with the protest, but the double-sided handbill, they said, was still a violation of the law. Chrestensen disagreed, began passing out his handbill, and was arrested. He then filed suit to enjoin the city from stopping him. The lower courts agreed with him that the law violated his First Amendment rights. But in a unanimous two-page decision in 1942, the Supreme Court reversed, holding that the city ordinance was permissible.

The Court said that the First Amendment does not prevent a city from regulating "purely commercial advertising." A city could regulate the purely commercial ads much more strictly than it could leaflets dealing with matters of public concern, such as notices of meetings and requests for religious donations. The Court hinted that there might also be some kinds of "purely commercial advertising" that nevertheless amounted to communications of public interest. But for many years no one, including the Court, picked up on this hint. So for a period of more than thirty years advertising seemed to be one kind of publication that, like "fighting words," lay beyond the protection of the First Amendment. But, as we will see in the next chapter, such a rigid interpretation proved to be impossible to maintain.

# 9.

## THE RIGHT
## TO ADVERTISE

### THE ABORTION CLINIC CASE

In 1971 the *Virginia Weekly*, a newspaper that circulated in Charlottesville, Virginia (especially on the campus of the University of Virginia), carried an advertisement for a New York abortion clinic. "UNWANTED PREGNANCY/LET US HELP YOU," read the headline. "Abortions are now legal in New York. There are no residency requirements," the ad went on to say, listing the address, telephone numbers, and further information about the New York City clinic. At that time not only were abortions unlawful in the State of Virginia, so were any advertisements that would "encourage or prompt" them. Jeffrey C. Bigelow, editor of the *Virginia Weekly*, was charged with violating the anti-advertising law and was convicted and sentenced to pay a fine of five hundred dollars.

Bigelow argued that the ad was purely informational. The Virginia Supreme Court thought otherwise. It said the ad "clearly exceeded" being informational and "constituted an active offer to perform a service, rather than a passive statement of fact." The state supreme court justified the anti-advertising law as designed to safeguard the interests of Virginia women: "to ensure that pregnant women in Virginia who decided to have abortions come to their decisions without the commercial advertising pressure usually incidental to the sale of a box of soap powder." The court pointed to the Chrestensen case as a precedent for the proposition that commercial advertising is not protected by the First Amendment. It also pointed to earlier U.S. Supreme Court decisions that upheld prohibitions against various types of advertisements related to the health-care industry, like ads for eyeglasses.

In 1975 the case came to the Supreme Court, which in a 7–2 decision reversed the state courts and held that such ads cannot be banned. Writing for the Court, Justice Blackmun denied "the central assumption made by the Supreme Court of Virginia . . . that the First Amendment guarantees of speech and press are inapplicable to paid commercial advertisements." The Chrestensen case, he said, was a very limited one. It was concerned only with the manner in which commercial advertising was distributed. It said nothing about the possibility of censoring or prohibiting commercial advertising altogether. Furthermore, all sorts of speech and writing have commercial motives. That books are sold in bookstores does not mean that the government can censor or ban them. A state cannot avoid the First Amendment "by mere labels," Justice Blackmun said.

The advertisement may not have been "purely informational" but it was not "purely commercial" either. Looking at the ad as a whole it "conveyed information of potential interest and value to a diverse audience. . . . The mere existence of the Women's Pavilion in New York City . . . and the availability of the services offered, were [newsworthy]." Additionally, the services, even though illegal in Virginia, were lawful in New York State. Virginia cannot outlaw conduct in New York or prevent its citizens from traveling to New York and using the services of the clinic in New York.

What was Virginia's interest in banning the ad? The state answered that if providers of medical services can advertise, then the quality of medical care may be adversely affected because people will tend to use the services they see advertised, and the doctors who do the advertising may be more interested in making money than in maintaining professional standards.

Justice Blackmun said that this interest was too thin to overcome the First Amendment. In the first place, no one claimed that the advertisement in any way lowered the quality of medical services in Virginia. In the second place, the state went after only the publisher of the newspaper, not the doctors, the clinic, or the advertising agency. Finally, none of the usual problems with ads was present: the ad was not deceptive or fraudulent, it did not advertise a service that was illegal, it invaded no one's privacy.

What was Virginia really doing? Justice Blackmun pointed out that it was "regulating what Virginians may *hear* or *read* about the New York services." In effect, the state was claiming that it could "shield its citizens from information about activities outside Virginia's borders." But if states were free to do this, then all sorts of information could be held up on similar grounds. Permitting such a thing to happen would seriously undermine the principles of free speech and free press, and the Court declined to permit it. Bigelow's conviction was overturned.

## THE DRUG PRICE ADVERTISING CASE

Bigelow's case tells us that if advertising contains a message of some public significance—something other than pure commercialism—it falls within the freedom of press. But is this the limit to the protection that advertisements have? May a state prohibit a purely commercial advertisement whenever the state doesn't like the commercial appeal? Less than one year after it dealt with the abortion clinic ad, the Supreme Court decided another Virginia advertising case, broadening considerably the legal protection given to ads.

The case involved a law prohibiting pharmacists from advertising drug prices. Under this Virginia law, any druggist who advertised the prices he charged for drugs could be fined or lose his license. The state argued that this law was essential to preserving the health of Virginia citizens. Allowing pharmacists to advertise would give an incentive to cut corners; with lower prices the druggists would have to sell more and be less careful about the way prescriptions were filled. Further, druggists who paid attention to individual customers and who needed higher prices to maintain this close relationship might lose long-time customers if price advertising caused prices to drop.

The Virginia Citizens Consumer Council, Inc., a non-profit association of drug consumers, felt that the law served a wholly different purpose: to keep prices artificially high. They had statistics that showed that drug prices varied widely within different areas in the state. For example, in the Newport News-Hampton area, an antibiotic drug called tetracycline ranged from $1.20 at some drugstores to $9.00 at others for the same quantity, a difference of 650 percent. (Such figures were not confined to Virginia; in Chicago, one study showed, drug price differences were as high as 1200 percent. In all, thirty-four states had similar laws forbidding drug price advertising.) The Consumer Council charged that the law served to inflate drug prices by keeping consumers in the dark. Without ads to call their attention to lower prices, many drugstores could get away with charging higher prices. After all, at the least it is a nuisance to make dozens of telephone calls to see which store has the lowest prices (and many druggists would not even give out prices on the telephone). But to shop from store to store all over town is time-consuming and expensive, and for many elderly people simply out of the question.

So the Consumer Council went to court to have the law upset as unconstitutional under the First Amendment. Their argument was simple: that in censoring the content of drug ads, even though "purely commercial," the State of Virginia was interfering with their right to *receive* important information.

The Supreme Court agreed. In an 8–1 decision, again written by Justice Blackmun, the Court said that to test the law it wasn't necessary for a druggist to go to court to assert his right to advertise. Those who read ads may also sue, because they have a First Amendment right "to receive information and ideas."

Justice Blackmun noted that the case clearly presented the issue of whether there is an exception in the First Amendment for "commercial speech." This was pure commercial speech, if ever there can be any: "our pharmacist does not wish to editorialize on any subject, cultural, philosophical, or political. He does not wish to report any particularly newsworthy fact, or to make generalized observations even about commercial matters. The 'idea' he wishes to communicate is simply this: 'I will sell you the X prescription drug at the Y price.'" But it is precisely this kind of statement, Justice Blackmun concluded, that the First Amendment protects.

In Thornhill's case (p. 51), no one argued that the strikers had to discuss the philosophy of unionism, rather than the particular labor dispute, to enjoy freedom of speech. As for the consumer, his interest in the "free flow of commercial information" may be even keener. Hardest hit are "the poor, the sick, and particularly the aged." They spend a greater proportion of their money on drugs, "yet they are the least able to learn, by shopping from pharmacist to pharmacist, where their scarce dollars are best spent." So they have a very important interest in learning the prices of drugs: "Information as to who is charging what becomes more than a convenience. It could mean the alleviation of physical pain or the enjoyment of basic necessities."

Finally, society as a whole has a strong interest in the free flow of commercial information. A free enterprise economy depends on "numerous private economic decisions. It is a matter of public interest that those decisions . . . be intelligent and well-informed." Without a free flow of all kinds of information, including commercial, the economy would become inefficient.

Against these considerations, Virginia's arguments about what advertising would do to pharmacists or the public did not amount to much, Justice Blackmun said. The most important reason Virginia's argument did not hold water is that druggists in that state, as in all states, are subject to a large number of regulations intended to preserve their professionalism. A druggist who "cuts corners" can be fined or lose his license anyway. The ban on advertising does not ensure that druggists will maintain their standards; it serves only to keep the public in ignorance. The state may regulate pharmacists, but not by the indirect approach of "keeping the public in ignorance of the entirely lawful terms that competing pharmacists are offering."

## THE SHAVED SANDPAPER CASE

That the First Amendment protects the right to advertise does not mean that it is all right to advertise in any manner whatsoever. Like "fighting words," *false* advertising is one class of thought that the First Amendment does not protect against government regulation.

Why false advertising? The First Amendment clearly protects "false opinions"—a statement that the President's plans for energy conservation are "terrible," for example, cannot serve as the basis for a criminal prosecution or a civil lawsuit, even if in fact the President's plans are not "terrible." In the realm of political affairs and public concerns, there is, as Justice Lewis F. Powell put it, "no such thing as a false idea."

But there are such things as "false facts": untrue statements that may mislead or deceive. To give misleading and deceptive advertising constitutional protection would mean that advertisers could lie about their products in order to make money that ought not be theirs. A fraudulent scheme should not be beyond the law's reach just because spoken or printed words are involved. Language is involved in all of human life, but that does not mean that there cannot be laws against criminal acts. People who plan together to commit a murder cannot escape responsibility for their actions by claiming that the First Amendment protects their right to talk to one another. So with advertising: the truth or falsity of the statements made is crucial to whether the ad has constitutional protection, as the "shaved sandpaper case" makes clear.

The case arose out of a television commercial prepared by an advertising agency for Colgate-Palmolive Company, makers of a shaving cream called Rapid Shave. Colgate-Palmolive claimed that Rapid Shave "outshaves them all." To demonstrate this, the advertising agency filmed commercials showing a razor shaving clean the surface of sandpaper. In this "sandpaper test" the announcer told the audience that "To prove Rapid Shave's super-moisturizing power, we put it right from the can onto this tough dry sandpaper. It was apply . . . soak . . . and off in a stroke." As the announcer spoke, the screen showed Rapid Shave being foamed onto a substance that looked like sandpaper. Immediately after, a razor whisked across the substance and shaved it clean.

But the substance was not sandpaper. It was a mock-up made of Plexiglas to which sand had been glued. The problem was that it took about eighty minutes for Rapid Shave to soak into real sandpaper. But eighty minutes is obviously too long to wait to dramatize a clean shave in seconds. Also, to say that it takes eighty minutes to soak in might suggest to potential users that they would have to wait that long with shaving cream on their faces. Finally, real sandpaper looked dull and flat on camera, like "plain colored paper." So although Rapid Shave really could shave sandpaper, Colgate-Palmolive agreed with its advertising agency to run the sixty-second commercial using the mock-up.

After conducting an investigation, the Federal Trade Commission (a federal agency empowered to put a stop to deceptive and misleading advertisements) concluded at the end of December 1961 that the commercial contained two misrepresentations of fact that amounted to deceptions to consumers. First, the commercial suggested that Rapid Shave could penetrate sandpaper in seconds, whereas in fact it could not. Second, it misled television viewers into thinking they were seeing sandpaper shaved, when in fact they were watching sand being removed from Plexiglas. The Commission ordered Colgate-Palmolive to "cease and desist" from using simulations in commercials in the future without advising viewers that what they were seeing was a mock-up.

The company appealed the FTC's order to a U.S. Court of Appeals. That court agreed that the false implication that Rapid Shave could shave sandpaper immediately on application was deceptive, and the company did not deny this. But the court agreed with the company that there was nothing wrong with the use of mock-ups about which viewers had not been told. The FTC appealed to the Supreme Court, which in a 7–2 decision reversed the lower court. It ruled that the failure to disclose the use of a mock-up was itself deceptive.

Writing for the majority, Chief Justice Warren noted that in connection with the mock-up the commercials made three representations to the viewing public:

(1) that sandpaper could be shaved by Rapid Shave;
(2) that an experiment had been conducted which verified this claim; and (3) that the viewer was seeing this experiment for himself.

It was clear that this last claim was false. The law prohibits making false claims about a product if they are a "material factor" in the decision to buy. Was this false claim the kind that a customer might want to know the truth about before deciding to buy the product? In many previous cases, the Supreme Court had ruled that false statements about the product or the company violated the law even if the customer was not particularly harmed by it. For example, in one case a company lied that its product normally sold for an inflated amount but that for a special sale the price was being reduced. Even though the customer was receiving his money's worth for the "reduced price"—which turned out to be the normal price—the Court had ruled that this was deceptive.

Colgate-Palmolive retorted that in the previous cases the

false statements were about the products. The use of a mock-up was not a false statement about Rapid Shave, since Rapid Shave really could shave sandpaper in exactly the way shown on the screen. The false statement was about whether the demonstration used sandpaper or Plexiglas, and Colgate-Palmolive wasn't selling either of those. So, it insisted, the lie didn't matter.

The company missed the point, the chief justice said. The demonstration was designed to convince viewers that they were seeing an actual test of the product. Like previous cases, including the case involving the inflated price, the deception relates to getting the customer to buy, not to how well the product actually works. The Court compared what Colgate-Palmolive did to a company's use of a famous person to endorse a product, knowing that the famous person doesn't even use the product. Obviously whether or not someone like Reggie Jackson uses Rapid Shave has no effect on the shaving cream, but to claim that he used it if he didn't would be deceptive.

Colgate-Palmolive also protested that it would be impractical to tell the viewing public about the mock-up. Chief Justice Warren said that the "ingenious advertising world" would undoubtedly be able to think of some way to tell the truth. But he then added a sentence which sums up the point, that false and deceptive advertisements are not protected by the First Amendment: "If, however, it becomes impossible or impractical to show simulated demonstrations on television in a truthful manner, this indicates that television is not a medium that lends itself to this type of commercial, not that the commercial must survive at all costs."

# 10.

## *DAMAGING A GOOD NAME*

False advertisements are not the only kind of untrue statements that can cause harm. Another category of harmful statements is slander (oral) and libel (written)—statements that injure a person's reputation, robbing him of or damaging his good name. Although one of the earliest free speech cases involved libel (recall that Governor Cosby accused John Peter Zenger of libel, p. 15), the law of libel did not meet up with the First Amendment until 1964, some 173 years after the Amendment was ratified. That is largely because libel has to do with *false* statements, and it was not considered necessary to give constitutional protection to false statements, which are like false advertisements and fighting words. In Zenger's case, remember, the government refused to let Andrew Hamilton show that what Zenger had said was true. In those days, truth was not a defense to a libel suit. Today it surely is.

During those 173 years, the law of libel became not only complex, as much law is, but also in many ways quite bizarre. Libel law varied from state to state and it grew up in a time before there were "mass media"—widely circulating newspapers and magazines, radio and television. Libel law was intended, instead, to protect a person against a neighbor or business acquaintance who might say nasty things about him. (If such comments found their way into a local newspaper, then the person whose reputation had been injured could sue the newspaper as well as the libeler.)

One of the major problems with the libel law was the set of rules governing proof of damages. If because of a libelous statement you lost your job, then you might sue to recover from the person who libeled you the amount of wages you missed until you found another job. But in most libel cases it is very difficult to prove in money terms how much injury has been done.

So a rule developed that if certain libels were made—for example, calling someone a criminal or saying that he was incompetent to perform his job—then the injured party wouldn't have to prove the extent of his injuries. He could simply ask the jury to recompense him for the harm in any amount the jurors thought fair. And if the plaintiff could show that the statement was made with "malice"—with evil intent to do harm—then he could ask for "punitive damages": an extra amount the jury might wish to award in order to punish the libeler.

However, if the libel was not obvious from the statement itself, but would only be taken as libelous by others who happened to know outside facts, then the law said that the injured plaintiff would have to show the actual extent of damages. The problem with rules such as these is that they set no standards for juries to follow, and can be used to seek huge sums of money from those whose intentions were innocent.

## THE CASE OF THE OFFENDED POLICE BOSS

The problems that libel law posed for the press became clear in a case involving the New York *Times* in the early 1960s. In its issue of March 29, 1960, the *Times* carried a fund-raising appeal in the form of an advertisement paid for by the Committee to Defend Martin Luther King and the Struggle for Freedom in the South. The ad's headline was: "Heed Their Rising Voices." Its message was that the efforts of "thousands of Southern Negro students" to overturn discriminatory laws and practices in the

South through non-violent demonstrations were "being met by an unprecedented wave of terror." In several paragraphs, the ad listed specific events to illustrate the "wave of terror." One of the paragraphs read as follows:

> In Montgomery, Alabama, after students sang "My Country, 'Tis of Thee" on the State Capitol steps, their leaders were expelled from school, and truckloads of police armed with shotguns and tear-gas ringed the Alabama State College Campus. When the entire student body protested to state authorities by refusing to re-register, their dining hall was padlocked in an attempt to starve them into submission.

The ad was signed by sixty-four persons well known in public affairs, religion, trade unions, and the performing arts, and carried a statement signed by twenty southern clergymen that they "warmly endorsed" the appeal for funds made in the ad.

The advertisement, it turned out, contained several errors. For example, the students had sung the "Star-Spangled Banner," not "My Country, 'Tis of Thee." Nine students had been expelled from school, but not for a demonstration on the Capitol steps; rather, for a lunch-counter demonstration on a different day. The entire student body had not protested, though most of it had, and they had not refused to register—they skipped class for a day. The dining hall had never been padlocked. There had been large numbers of police but they did not ring the campus.

During part of the time talked about in the ad, one L. B. Sullivan was Commissioner of Public Affairs of the City of Montgomery. Among his duties was supervision of the police department. He claimed that he had been libeled by the statements in the ad, even though he was never mentioned by name. His theory was that people would read the word "police" as referring to him. People would think he was the person responsible for doing the acts mentioned. His personal reputation suffered thereby, he asserted. He filed suit for libel in an Alabama court against the New York *Times* and four of the signers.

At the trial, Sullivan put witnesses on the stand who testified that they "would not want to be associated with anybody who would be a party to such things as are stated in that ad." A former employer of Sullivan testified that he would not rehire Sullivan if the statements were true. But no witness told the jury that he actually believed any of the statements were true. (What difference does it make whether the witnesses believed the statements to be false? The answer is that if everyone assumed the statements to be false, then the plaintiff could not claim to be injured.) Nor did Sullivan offer any proof of how much in money terms his reputation had suffered.

The *Times* testified that the ad cost $4800. The ad was placed through an agency acting for the committee, which forwarded a letter from its chairman, A. Philip Randolph, a nationally known civil rights activist. The *Times* has an advertising acceptability department that tries to weed out claims for products that are clearly false or in bad taste. But the head of the department testified that since Randolph was known to be a responsible person, the paper was content to accept his word that the ad was properly authorized by the committee and its signers. Having "no reason to question" the content of the ad, the paper made no effort to confirm the accuracy of the statements made in the ad.

Even though there was no reference to Sullivan anywhere in the ad, the Alabama jury sided with Sullivan and awarded him a $500,000 judgment. The judge instructed the jury that Sullivan did not have to prove how much the statements injured him. The judge also said that the jury could award punitive damages if it wished.

The Alabama Supreme Court upheld the jury verdict and denied that it had been excessive. The court said that the jury could have inferred malice from the *Times's* "irresponsibility" in failing to check its own files for the facts in the news stories it had printed about the civil rights protests in Alabama. The state supreme court also said that the First Amendment did not apply, for two reasons: (1) because the Amendment protects the freedom of the press only from actions of the government, whereas here Sullivan was suing as a private party; and (2) because the libelous statement was contained in a commercial advertisement.

In a unanimous decision, the U.S. Supreme Court reversed the state court and tossed out Sullivan's suit. The Court made several points, in an opinion by Justice William Brennan.

First, this was not a case of private action but of clear governmental action. Unlike many of the other cases we have examined, however, the governmental body that was abridging the freedom of the press was not the executive branch (police chiefs, city managers, governors) nor the legislature, but the courts themselves. For it was the Alabama trial court that used certain rules of libel to reach a verdict against the *Times*.

Second, it was irrelevant that the alleged libel appeared in a commercial advertisement. The Court said that the Chrestensen case (p. 81) was not a precedent for the Sullivan case, because the statements in the civil rights ad were matters of public concern.

Third—and now the Court reached the core of the case— Justice Brennan observed that because the advertisement concerned "one of the major public issues of our time," the statements clearly "qualify for the constitutional protection" of the First Amendment, unless their falsity can overcome that protection. If falsity alone were enough to overcome the First Amendment, this very case showed the consequences: in the absence of any proof that Sullivan had actually been injured, he was awarded a sum 1000 times greater than the Alabama code set as a maximum fine for someone who violated a law against maliciously and falsely calling someone a criminal (Sullivan had won $500,000; the maximum state fine would have been $500). Moreover, others in the police department might make the same claims and bring similar lawsuits. One large award is bad enough, but several would obviously intimidate any newspaper into printing nothing but the safest and least controversial news.

But shouldn't people pay for their failure to check the accuracy of the statements they make or allow to be printed? No, said Justice Brennan, not if the mistake was honestly made—that is, if it was made without deliberate intent to injure. That is partly because it is impossible to check every fact every day, especially in fast-moving situations, and partly because it is so often difficult actually to prove "truth" in a courtroom according to legal rules. Said Justice Brennan: "A rule compelling the critic of official conduct to guarantee the truth of all his factual assertions—and to do so on pain of libel judgments virtually unlimited in amount—leads to . . . self-censorship. . . . Under such a rule, would-be critics of official conduct may be deterred from voicing their criticism, even though it is believed to be true and even though it is in fact true, because of doubt whether it can be proved in court or fear of the expense of having to do so. [A libel suit these days can easily cost $100,000 or more to defend.] . . . The rule thus dampens the vigor and limits the variety of public debate."

So the Alabama libel law, the Court concluded, was much too restrictive. In its place, the Court announced a new rule in its 1964 decision in *New York Times v. Sullivan*: a public official cannot sue for libel about his official conduct unless he can prove that the statement was made with what the Court called "actual malice." Actual malice, the Court said, means that the publisher printed a false statement either "[1] with knowledge that it was false or [2] with reckless disregard of whether it was false or not."

Having thus set forth a new rule of libel, applicable in all states across the country, the Court went on to examine the particulars in Sullivan's case against the *Times*. The Court concluded that even if there were to be a new trial at which the new rule was followed, Sullivan could not win. There were two principal reasons. First, the *Times*'s failure to check its files for the accuracy of the facts in the advertisement was not an act done "with knowledge" of falsity or "with reckless disregard of whether it was false or not." The *Times* acted in reasonable reliance on the word of a responsible person. Second, in any event there was no reasonable way to connect the statements in the ad with Commissioner Sullivan. His name was never used, and even under traditional libel law a person cannot claim to have been libeled unless the reference to him is clear enough for most people to see that the statements apply to him personally.

## THE CASE OF THE LIBELED LAWYER

As important as the Sullivan case was, it was only a beginning. It left many unanswered questions. Sullivan was a public official, elected by the people of Montgomery. Statements concerning the actions of the police obviously dealt with the official duties of public officeholders. Who else besides public officials might fall within the rule in Sullivan's case, and for what actions?

Only a few months after the Court decided the Sullivan case, it handed down another decision extending the reach of the Sullivan rule. The District Attorney of New Orleans got into a dispute with eight judges of the criminal district court. He held a press conference and denounced the judges, among other things charging that their failure to authorize him to spend public funds for certain investigations "raises interesting questions about the racketeer influences on our eight vacation-minded judges."

The district attorney was prosecuted on criminal charges (as Zenger was) under an old Louisiana law that permitted criminal trials for certain kinds of libel. The Supreme Court reversed his conviction, again unanimously and again in an opinion by Justice Brennan. The judges who claimed to have been libeled argued that the district attorney's remarks were related to their private lives, not covered by the Court's earlier decision in the Sullivan case. But the Court disagreed. Said Justice Brennan: "Where the criticism is of public officials and their conduct of public business, the interest in private reputation is overborne by the larger public interest, secured by the Constitution, in the dissemination of truth." Furthermore, the district attorney's personal anger and hostility were not enough to prove "malice" under the First Amendment. Libel cannot be proved simply by showing that the defendant had ill-will toward the plaintiff. There must be proof that the defendant made a statement that he knew to be false or that he recklessly disregarded the likelihood that what he said was false. "Even if he did speak out of hatred," the Court said, "utterances honestly believed contribute to the free interchange of ideas and the ascertainment of truth."

It is important to be able to discuss freely the conduct of government through its officials, without fearing that they will sue whenever someone says or prints something about them or about what they have done. But officials are not the only group of people it is important to discuss and debate. For example, someone while running for public office may not actually hold any office (when Jimmy Carter ran for President in 1976 he was a private citizen). Should that make a difference? Should a private citizen much in the public eye be able to sue, whereas a public official may not? In several cases during the 1960s and early 1970s the Supreme Court extended the Sullivan rule to protect stories about public figures and public events.

But that still leaves one class of people: individuals who are neither public officials nor public figures. A private citizen about whom the press prints false stories that injure his reputation may certainly recover damages if the press acted with knowledge that the stories were false or acted in reckless disregard of their falsity. But that is a difficult burden for a plaintiff to prove, as it was designed to be. So the question is whether the private individual ought to have a lesser burden: whether he can recover damages when the press was only careless about what it did. In 1974, ten years after the Sullivan case, the Supreme Court in a 5–4 decision ruled that the private individual indeed ought to have an easier time in proving his case.

The facts in the case were simple. In 1968, a Chicago policeman named Nuccio shot and killed a young man named Nelson.
Nuccio was convicted of murder. The Nelson family hired Elmer
Gertz, a well-known Chicago lawyer, to sue Nuccio in civil
court for Nelson's death. *American Opinion,* a monthly journal
of the John Birch Society, did not like what was happening to
Nuccio. For years this right-wing magazine had been claiming
that there was a conspiracy to destroy local police forces in order
to make way for a communist takeover. The Nuccio case was
an example, the editor thought. He ran a story in the March 1969
issued entitled "FRAME-UP: Richard Nuccio and the War On
Police." In this article, the author asserted that the testimony
at Nuccio's murder trial was false, cooked up as part of a communist plot. Gertz, the Nelson family's lawyer, had played no
part in the criminal trial. Nevertheless, the *American Opinion*
article portrayed him as central to the "frame-up." The article
called him a "Leninist" and a "Communist-fronter." It also said
that he had a criminal record. None of these charges was true.

Gertz filed suit for libel against *American Opinion.* The
magazine responded in two ways. First, it said that Gertz was a
public figure as a well-known lawyer, author, and lecturer who
had been involved in matters of public importance. Second, the
magazine said that even if Gertz was not a public figure, the
subject of frame-ups of the police and the lawsuits concerning
Nuccio were matters of public interest. That was enough, the
magazine argued, to bring the Sullivan rule into play. That in
turn meant that Gertz would have to show that the editors either
knew the libelous statements to be false or else were reckless
in disregarding the probability that they were false. But that
couldn't be shown in this case, the magazine argued, because
the editor of the article had relied on his prior experience with
the writer of the piece, an outside contributor who had written
other stories for the magazine. The editor himself knew nothing about the facts in dispute and could not be expected to
know them.

The lower courts agreed and dismissed Gertz's lawsuit. The

Supreme Court disagreed and reinstated it, ruling that Gertz was a private individual, not a public figure, and had not thrust himself into the limelight. It is of great social importance to have a Sullivan rule to prevent self-censorship of the press, but that is not the only social value, the Court said. "There is no constitutional value in false statements of fact," Justice Powell declared in the majority opinion, adding that the press ought not to escape liability for libeling a private person. The First Amendment imposes a limitation on the power of states to award libel judgments, but the First Amendment does not prohibit all libel judgments.

Why draw a line between public officials and figures on the one hand, and private individuals on the other? One reason is that public figures and individuals generally have an easier time of correcting falsehoods. Newspapers will print their denials and television stations will put them on the air to defend themselves. Private individuals usually have much more difficulty in doing so. Another reason is that people who are in the public eye usually have sought to be there and must accept the consequences of the occasional falsehood in the heat of public debate. But private individuals have not sought publicity and they ought not to be penalized when their reputations are attacked. So the Court ruled that each state may set its own rule for deciding under what circumstances the press must pay for libeling a private individual.

The Court's ruling was not all on the side of the individual and against the press. The Court balanced its decision by limiting the kind of damages that can be awarded. This was a substantial victory for the press. The Court said that a private individual who wins a libel suit cannot collect a sum of money in excess of his actual damages. That is, the plaintiff can no longer simply point to the libelous statement and ask the jury for a sum of money. He must show how and to what extent he was injured. Moreover, the jury cannot award punitive damages unless there really was malice as the Court defined it in the Sullivan case. Only if the press knowingly prints a falsehood or recklessly ignores the likelihood that the statement is false can the plaintiff collect an extra-large judgment. Otherwise juries would "remain free to use their discretion selectively to punish expressions of unpopular views."

## THE CASE OF THE ANGUISHED FATHER

Libel deals with false statements that unfairly harm a person's reputation. As we have just seen, libelous statements, like "fighting words," are not protected by the First Amendment—though the First Amendment does give "breathing room" to many kinds of false statements about public officials and public figures. But what about *true* statements? There are certain kinds of truths that hurt as much as any kind of false statement. Governor Cosby was stung by Zenger's charges—truths about the royal governor's greed and corruption. That kind of truth we know the First Amendment will not let be suppressed, for that kind of truth concerns the most vital public matters: the conduct of the government by government officials. Cosby's acts concerned and affected the public. But the acts of most people do not affect the public. Most people live private lives. Can they prevent the press from publishing true details of their lives?

This question was tested in a Georgia case in 1975. In August 1971, seventeen-year-old Cynthia Cohn was raped and killed by six teenagers in Sandy Springs, Georgia. There was considerable newspaper coverage of the crime but the victim's name was not reported, apparently because of a Georgia statute that made it a misdemeanor to publish or broadcast the name or identity of a rape victim. In April 1972 the defendants appeared in court. Five of the youths pleaded guilty and one pleaded not guilty. Trial of this last defendant was set for another day.

On the day the five pleaded guilty, a television reporter named Wassell learned the name of the victim. This he did by the simple method of asking court officials to see copies of the indictments (the official papers charging the defendants with the crimes). The indictments, as required by law, listed Cynthia Cohn as the victim and stated the details of the crimes that the state would endeavor to prove. The court clerk who showed the indictments to Wassell made no attempt to cover up the name, nor did he tell Wassell he could not use it. Later that day Wassell broadcast the name over WSB-TV during his report on the court proceedings, and he repeated the name the next day during a follow-up report.

Martin Cohn, Cynthia's father, sued Cox Broadcasting Corporation, owner of WSB-TV, for invasion of his privacy. Although the legal issues were complex (for example, is the mentioning of a deceased daughter's name an invasion of the *father's* privacy?) the Georgia Supreme Court ultimately ruled that the First Amendment does not stand in the way of a trial. The court said that the name of a rape victim was not matter of public concern and the press could be penalized for mentioning it. In a nutshell, Cohn was asserting that he had a "right to be free from unwanted publicity about his private affairs, which, although wholly true, would be offensive to a person of ordinary sensibilities." The television station, on the other hand, argued that it had an absolute right to broadcast accurate statements, no matter how embarrassing or painful they might be to a private individual.

In an 8–1 decision handed down in 1975, the U.S. Supreme Court ruled in favor of Cox Broadcasting Corp. In his majority opinion, Justice White emphasized that the case concerned broadcasting of a name obtained from public records, which themselves were open to public inspection. Anyone who wanted to know Cynthia Cohn's name could have gone to the courthouse and looked at the indictments. When the state put this information on public record, it must have concluded that the information was of interest and concern to the public. Said White: "Public records by their very nature are of interest to those concerned with the administration of government, and a public benefit is performed by the reporting of the true contents of the records. . . . The freedom of the press to publish that information appears to us to be of critical importance to our type of government in which the citizenry is the final judge of the proper conduct of public business. . . . [The First Amendment commands] nothing less than that the States may not impose sanctions for the publication of truthful information contained in official court records open to public inspection." The rule that Martin Cohn wanted, Justice White said, would inevitably lead to self-censorship, because who is to say in any given case what a man of "ordinary sensibilities" would want kept private?

Notice what the Court did not say. It did not say that television stations may broadcast *any* true facts. The decision was limited to facts in public records open for public inspection. If the State of Georgia had itself kept Cynthia Cohn's name private and the reporter had stolen the court papers or in some other unlawful manner discovered the name, then it might have been possible to sue for invasion of privacy. But Wassell obtained the name in a lawful manner, and his station's right to broadcast the name was thus upheld.

# 11.

## *TABOO TOPICS*

What the First Amendment protects, it protects virtually absolutely. But some types of expression—fighting words, incitements to immediate violence, libel—do not fall within the First Amendment's protective shield. Drawing the lines between permissible expression and the few types that are not is a delicate business. But in these areas it is clear that the line that is finally drawn circumscribes a very small area of impermissible speech. We now turn to a different kind of problem: broader types of speech that many people consider "taboo"—topics that they would like to forbid us to read or watch or sell.

### SACRILEGE

In 1950 Roberto Rossellini's forty-minute film *The Miracle* opened at a theater in New York City. It was an Italian film about a demented girl (powerfully acted by the celebrated actress Anna Magnani) who tended goats on a mountainside. She becomes pregnant and thinks that she, like the Virgin Mary, is carrying the Son of God. The village people taunt her and abuse her until finally she runs off to live in a cave. She gives birth, alone, inside a church, calling out to God, and when she hears the cries of her child she regains her sanity.

Under the laws of New York, the State Education Department

had to license a film before it could be shown. The exhibitors received the license and the film played for about eight weeks. During this time a great controversy arose: many protested the showing on the ground that it was "sacrilegious." This term originally referred to the crime of stealing from a church, but in modern times it has come to mean the saying or doing of something that insults, mocks, or scorns a sacred belief.

Although a large number of critics praised the film, and although most of those connected with making the film were Catholic, Francis Cardinal Spellman of New York condemned it and called on "all right thinking citizens" to unite to tighten censorship laws. In mid-February, 1951, the state licensing agency reconsidered its position and rescinded the film's license, saying that the "mockery or profaning of these beliefs that are sacred to any portion of our citizenship is abhorrent to the laws of this great State." The licensing authority's withdrawal of approval to show the film was upheld by the highest court of New York as not a violation of the First Amendment.

In 1952 the case came to the Supreme Court, which unanimously reversed the decision of the New York courts. The State had argued that movies are not entitled to constitutional protection because their exhibition is done for business reasons. Movies ought not be considered part of the press, the State said. Writing for the majority, Justice Tom C. Clark said that New York was wrong: "It cannot be doubted that motion pictures are a significant medium for the communication of ideas. They may affect public attitudes and behavior in a variety of ways, ranging from direct espousal of a political or social doctrine to the subtle shaping of thought which characterizes all artistic expression." That movies are designed to entertain does not make a legal difference: "What is one man's amusement, teaches another's doctrine." Finally, most forms of the press—newspapers, magazines, and books—are sold for a profit, but that does not rob them of the First Amendment's protection. So for the first time, the Supreme Court declared that motion pictures are shielded by the First Amendment.

But the Court also tossed out New York's theory that certain taboo topics—like expressions of sacrilege—can be banned. What meaning can be given to such a term? The New York Court of Appeals, the state's highest court, had said that there is "nothing mysterious" about the law prohibiting sacrilege. "It is simply this: that no religion, as that word is understood by the ordinary, reasonable person, shall be treated with contempt, mockery, scorn and ridicule . . . by those engaged in selling entertainment by way of motion pictures." But this definition, said Justice Clark, is not a narrow exception to the First Amendment; it is a very broad one: "The censor is set adrift upon a boundless sea amid a myriad of conflicting currents of religious views, with no charts but those provided by the most vocal and powerful orthodoxies." The censor would sooner or later wind up banning "the expression of unpopular sentiments" that remain "sacred to a religious minority." But "it is not the business of government in our nation to suppress real or imagined attacks upon a particular religious doctrine, whether they appear in publications, speeches, or motion pictures."

Although Justice Clark did not refer to the Zenger case, it is interesting to recall that Andrew Hamilton had pointed out the irony that blasphemous comments (profaning the name of God) could circulate freely in the colonies whereas true statements about one's earthly governors could not. It was remarkable that more than two hundred years later New York was trying to restore some protection to God, who presumably does not need it.

In a thirty-three-page "concurring" opinion (one in which a judge agrees with the result of the case, though not necessarily with the reasons), Justice Frankfurter set forth in detail evidence showing the vagueness of the term "sacrilege." The New York courts assumed that the term had a definite meaning, but Justice Frankfurter showed in eight pages of history and by quoting seven pages' worth of dictionary definitions that the term in theory—and in practice—meant all kinds of different things to different people. Since vague laws inevitably promote self-censorship by the press, to avoid coming too close to whatever it was that the legislature intended to outlaw, the licensing law of New York was clearly invalid, Frankfurter said.

## OBSCENITY

In the sacrilege case, Justice Clark noted at the end of the opinion that the Court was not that day thinking about a separate issue: whether a state may censor motion pictures under a carefully written law designed to eliminate obscenity. When the issue did arise five years later, in 1957, the Supreme Court ruled in a 7–2 decision that obscene publications, whether books or magazines or movies, are not protected by the First Amendment.

The decision came in two cases joined together. In one, a man named Roth was convicted of mailing from New York obscene material through the U.S. postal system, in violation of federal law. In the other case, a man named Alberts, who ran a mail-order business in Los Angeles, was convicted of violating a state law against offering obscene material for sale.

Justice Brennan wrote the majority decision. He began by noting that at the time the First Amendment was adopted, no one believed that it protected obscenity. From the earliest days of the nation, obscenity was rejected "as utterly without redeeming social importance." The purpose of the First Amendment is to promote discussion of ideas of all sorts. But, as the Court noted earlier in Chaplinsky's case (p. 44), obscene "utterances are no essential part of any exposition of ideas, and are of such slight social value as a step to truth that any benefit that may be derived from them is clearly outweighed by the social interest in order and morality."

As with libel and incitements to violence, it is difficult to determine what is in fact obscene, for obscenity is no more precise a term than sacrilege. For fifteen years, for example, James Joyce's *Ulysses*, one of the greatest novels in the English language, was banned from the United States as obscene, until a federal judge in New York in 1933 upset the postal regulations as applied to that book (the case was never appealed to the Supreme Court). And over the years many classics, including Ernest Hemingway's *The Sun Also Rises*, Theodore Dreiser's *An American Tragedy*, Sinclair Lewis's *Elmer Gantry*, Mark Twain's *Huckleberry Finn*, have been banned in one state or another. By the standards of our day, these books are so tame that it is difficult to understand what the fuss was all about. (In a few towns, more recent novels, such as Joseph Heller's *Catch-22*, Piri Thomas's *Down These Mean Streets*, and Kurt Vonnegut's *Cat's Cradle*, have been yanked off public library shelves as obscene.)

Nor has censorship under obscenity laws been confined to novels. Non-fiction books too have suffered, including medical books and, in one astonishing case, a book of philosophy by the distinguished British philosopher Bertrand Russell. That is the difficulty with laws permitting censors to ban books for obscenity: it is too easy for a group of people who dislike an author, a theme, an idea, or a philosophy to press criminal charges against authors, publishers, and booksellers, either to punish them for having written something that offends the group or to scare off others with similar thoughts. This is the essence of censorship, and allowing obscenity to stand as an exception to the First Amendment poses a threat to the freedom of the press.

But even if obscenity laws are not directed against books on political or social themes, they still pose difficulties, as Justice Douglas pointed out in his dissent. In the Roth case, the trial judge told the jury that the federal postal statute outlaws literature dealing with sex if it offends "the common conscience of the community." Said Douglas: "Certainly that standard would not be an acceptable one if religion, economics, politics or philosophy were involved. How does it become a constitutional standard when literature treating with sex is concerned?"

Justice Harlan dissented in the Roth case on the ground that the First Amendment prohibits *federal* laws against obscenity, while permitting *state* laws to deal with it. For one state to classify a book as obscene does not prevent another state from letting it circulate. But "the dangers to free thought and expression are truly great if the Federal Government imposes a blanket ban over the Nation on such a book. The prerogative of the States to differ on their ideas of morality will be destroyed, the ability of States to experiment will be stunted. The fact that the people of one State cannot read some of the works of D. H. Lawrence [*Lady Chatterley's Lover* had been banned in several states] seems to me, if not wise or desirable, at least acceptable. But that no person in the United States should be allowed to do so seems to me to be intolerable, and violative of both the letter and spirit of the First Amendment."

However, in upholding the power of both federal and state governments to legislate against obscenity, the Supreme Court did not say that "anything goes." A state may not prosecute a bookseller or publisher if a book contains a few offensive four-letter words. A book must be judged as a whole, and it must be judged by "contemporary community standards," not the standards of the most squeamish person in town.

The Roth and Alberts cases did not stop the controversy over the obscenity issue. In fact, this was the first time the Supreme Court had ruled on the issue, and it proved to be only the beginning of the debate. Since its decision in 1957, several important cases have not been consistently decided. The rules that the Court has laid down from time to time were not then and still are not clear—in 1966, in three separate cases decided the same day, there were fourteen separate opinions of the justices!—and in any event the rules are too complex to be discussed here in detail.

During the 1960s, the Supreme Court struck down several state obscenity convictions without writing opinions. The Court also tightened its definition of obscenity to such a degree that for a time it seemed as though, as a practical matter, the issue was dead. Only materials "*utterly* without redeeming social importance" were unprotected by the First Amendment, and the standard had to be a national one. A judge or jury in a small town in states hostile to much modern literature could not say "*we* think this book is utterly without redeeming social importance"; instead, any jury would have to decide whether people generally throughout the United States thought so. In 1969 the Court ruled that in the privacy of one's home obscene materials—by any definition—could be read.

But in 1973 the Court shifted direction. With several new justices now on the Court (Justices Black and Harlan had died, Chief Justice Warren had retired), the Court in a 5–4 decision seemed to back away from the generally permissive direction it had taken in the 1960s. In its 1973 decision the Court gave local juries much more leeway to find particular works obscene. But still the rules were not clear. Indeed, the very next year the justices had to spend time in still another decision explaining what it meant in the 1973 decision.

Although the law of obscenity is always subject to change, it continues to be the law that obscenity is not protected by the First Amendment. It appears to be the law that only works which today are loosely referred to as "hard core" may constitutionally be banned. Not every library board or local prosecutor has received this message yet, however, and more cases are sure to come to state courts and ultimately to the nine justices of the Supreme Court, who for this purpose sit as the ultimate board of censors.

# 12.

## FAIR TRIAL— FREE PRESS

In recent years, one of the most aggravated free press issues has concerned newspaper, radio, and television coverage of pending trials. The Sixth Amendment to the Constitution, which is certainly not inferior to the First, guarantees to those accused of crime the right to a fair trial, which includes the right to an impartial judge and jury. But it is hard to remain impartial when a case is making headline news. Even if the news reports show no bias, they may contaminate the minds of potential jurors with erroneous or true but irrelevant information. Such news stories help sell newspapers and keep the viewers tuned in to television news coverage, and often contain important information the public has a right to know. To stop the press from publishing anything about a case that is coming to court would deprive us not only of interesting news but frequently of the most urgent and vital news.

In England, where there is no First Amendment, the press must cease publishing stories about any matter that goes to court. The penalty for violating this rule is "contempt of court," which is punishable by stiff monetary fines and, in an aggravated case, by a jail sentence for an editor or publisher. The sad fact is, however, that without a probing press the public lacks knowledge of how well the courts are handling the issues that come before them. Often great injustice has been done in important cases because too many facts can be kept secret in a courtroom closed to the press—and because not knowing those facts, others outside the courtroom cannot independently begin to remedy the injustice or be pushed into doing so.

Because we do have a First Amendment in the United States, the general rule, as you would expect, is that the press may not be held in contempt for publishing stories about trials, defendants, judges, lawyers, or court personnel. When it sometimes happens that there has been an overwhelming amount of publicity unfair to the defendant (an occasionally sensationalist press is the price of the First Amendment), convictions have been overturned and new trials ordered to take place in a different city or county.

Judges also can and do order participants in the trial not to talk to the press. These orders, which increased in number during the 1970s, are usually called "gag orders," because they gag the mouths of the parties, witnesses, and lawyers. Because they directly impinge on the right to speak they are controversial, but they are generally upheld as necessary to ensure a fair trial.

But contempt citations and gag orders directed against the press are not constitutional, and though judges occasionally try to gag the press or find it in contempt, they are not successful because of the following two cases.

## THE CASE OF THE INTIMIDATED JUDGE

Labor problems brought this case to a head. In the midst of a strike marred by violence, two union members in Los Angeles were convicted in 1938 of assaulting a non-union truck driver. The defendants asked the court to sentence them to probation instead of to jail. Judge A. A. Scott of Los Angeles Superior Court set a day in June for ruling on their requests and pronouncing sentence. About a month before that date, on May 5, 1938, the Los Angeles *Times* wrote a scathing editorial condemning the perpetrators of labor violence and ridiculing the defendants' pleas for lenience. The last paragraph of the editorial read as follows:

> It will teach no lesson to other thugs to put these men on good behavior for a limited time. Their "duty" would simply be taken over by others like them. If [these] thugs, however, are made to realize that they face San Quentin when they are caught, it will tend to make their disreputable occupation unpopular. Judge A. A. Scott will make a serious mistake if he grants probation to Matthew Shannon and Kennan Holmes. This community needs the example of their assignment to the jute mill [jail].

For this and for two other editorials the *Times* published, the company that owned the newspaper and the *Times*'s managing editor were cited for contempt of court and fined. The fine for the editorial quoted above was three hundred dollars. There was no statute authorizing such a citation or punishment in these circumstances. The *Times* asserted that the contempt citation was a violation of the First Amendment. But the Superior Court, which handed down the contempt citation, and the California Supreme Court denied that it was. These courts reasoned that they had "inherent" power to provide fair trials—that even without legislative approval they had the power as courts to do so. They reasoned that to provide a fair trial it would be necessary to take appropriate measures to prevent judges from being "coerced" or "intimidated." In their judgment, the editorial saying that Judge Scott would "make a serious mistake" if he were to grant probation was an act of intimidation, because it put pressure on him to sentence the two men to jail—or feel the wrath of public opinion if he decided, contrary to the wisdom of the Los Angeles *Times*, to grant probation anyway. So, the courts went on to say, they could use their time-honored power to punish for contempt to deter others in the future from interfering in the administration of justice by commenting on pending litigation.

By a 5–4 vote in 1941, the Supreme Court reversed the contempt citation. In an opinion by Justice Black, the majority said that courts do not have an independent power, lying outside the reach of the First Amendment, to punish those who print stories or editorials that judges do not like or that they fear. To hold that there is an exception to the First Amendment in the case of comment on public trials and legal proceedings would be to make a serious inroad on the principles of press freedom. The California courts conceded that they could not punish a newspaper for commenting on a case after it was all finished. But cases drag on often for long periods of time, and allowing courts to censor the press while cases are pending would not be a limited or insignificant abridgement of freedom of expression. Such a rule would mean that the press could be constantly halted from talking about issues of great public moment.

There also cannot be an exception to the First Amendment in order to protect the judiciary from public disrespect. "It is a prized American privilege," Justice Black said, "to speak one's mind, although not always with perfect good taste, on all public institutions. And an enforced silence, however limited, solely in the name of preserving the dignity of the bench, would probably engender resentment, suspicion, and contempt much more than it would enhance respect."

The contempt citation, then, could only be upheld in the face of the First Amendment if there had been a "clear and present danger" of serious disruption to the administration of justice. Was there such a threat in this case?

Indeed not, said Justice Black. To begin with, it was "inconceivable" that any judge in Los Angeles would expect anything but criticism from the Los Angeles *Times* if probation were granted in this case, in view of the paper's long-standing editorial position. But nobody doubted that an editorial *after* sentencing would have been proper. So what did this editorial, published a month *before* the sentencing, really do? At most, it "did no more than threaten future adverse criticism which was reasonably to be expected anyway in the event of a lenient disposition of the pending case. To regard it, therefore, as in itself of substantial influence upon the court of justice would be to impute to judges a lack of firmness, wisdom, or honor, which we cannot accept."

Since this 1941 case, a handful of others have come to the Supreme Court in which newspapers have been held in contempt for publishing articles or editorials critical of judges, but the Court has never sustained a single contempt citation. Judges, no more than any other public servant, are not beyond criticism where the First Amendment lives.

### THE GAG ORDER CASE

On October 18, 1975, police in Sutherland, Nebraska, a small town of only 850 people, discovered the bodies of six members of the Henry Kellie family in their home. They had been murdered. The police released a picture of Erwin Charles Simants, a suspect, to local reporters who had gathered at the Kellie home. The next morning Simants was arrested and brought to jail, "ending a tense night for this small rural community."

Immediately the crime brought reporters from local, regional, and national newspapers and radio and television stations hurrying to Sutherland. Stories about the crime, the Kellie family, the town, and Simants quickly spread to the public. Three days later the county attorney, who would be in charge of prosecuting Simants for murder, and Simants' own lawyer asked the county court for a "restrictive" (gag) order concerning what the press could and could not report. This was necessary, they argued, because of the "mass coverage by news media" and the "reasonable likelihood of prejudicial news which would make difficult, if not impossible, the impaneling of an impartial jury and tend to prevent a fair trial." The next day the county judge issued an order forbidding anyone who attended any public hearing in the case from reporting any testimony given or evidence shown. That very day a hearing was held and reporters were permitted to attend but they were told they were bound by the court's order.

Several press and broadcast associations, publishers, and individual reporters then went to a higher court, asking that the gag order be "vacated" (annulled). The court heard arguments and then issued its own order. This new order prohibited the press from reporting six things:

1. The existence and contents of a confession that Simants had made to police officers, and which was brought out in open court at the hearing a few days before.

2. The fact of Simants' having made statements to others and the nature of those statements.

3. The contents of a note he wrote the night of the crime.

4. Parts of medical testimony at the hearing.

5. The identity of victims of an assault and the nature of the assault.

6. The nature of the gag order itself. (Obviously, if the press could report that the judge had refused to let it print information concerning a confession, people would at least know that there was a confession. At that time, the existence of a confession was exactly what the judge was trying to avoid making public. Whether or not confessions should be admitted into evidence at a criminal trial is a very delicate and complex legal question. If potential jurors knew in advance that there was a confession, the decision to keep it out of evidence would not mean much and would therefore interfere with the defendant's right to a fair trial.)

The press associations and other journalists took their case to the Nebraska Supreme Court. Moving swiftly, that court heard arguments and on December 2, about six weeks after the crime, handed down its decision. The court recognized the legal difficulty in imposing a prior restraint on the press. At the same time, it said, both society and the defendant had a vital interest in assuring trial by an impartial jury. The extensive publicity surrounding the case jeopardized this right. Under state law, Simants had to be tried within six months and even if the trial were to be moved outside of the county where the crime occurred, it could only be moved to a neighboring county. Everyone in the area was subject to the same publicity.

The state supreme court took a compromise position. It modified the lower court's order so that only three topics could not be reported: (1) all matters relating to a confession to the police; (2) all matters relating to any statements Simants might have made to others; and (3) other facts "strongly implicative" of the accused (that is, facts that would suggest to a potential juror his probable guilt).

Under the terms of the state court's decision, the gag order expired automatically on January 7, 1976, when a jury was chosen. Until that time, the press could not print some of what it wanted to print. After that time, it could and did. Simants was convicted of murder and sentenced to death. But the press associations and other journalists who had gone to the state supreme court pressed an appeal to the United States Supreme Court.

Since the trial was already over, why did they press this appeal? For one thing, there was always a chance that Simants' conviction would be upset on appeal to a state court. If he were to be retried, a gag order might be imposed again. But even if this didn't happen, the state court decision was an important precedent. For both reasons, the journalists were anxious to overturn it.

The U.S. Supreme Court agreed to hear the case and six months later, in June 1976, unanimously reversed the state courts. The gag order, the Court said in an opinion by Chief Justice Burger, was unconstitutional.

There is no question, the chief justice began, that the right to a fair trial by an impartial jury is an exceedingly important one in our society. That is why on several occasions the Supreme Court itself has reversed criminal convictions solely on the ground that there had been too much sensational, "carnival-like" publicity at the time of the trial. (In one case the defendant's "highly emotional" confession had actually been shown on television three times prior to his trial.) But to say that the defendant has such

a right does not mean that the only way to protect it is to prohibit the press from publishing.

In this case, Chief Justice Burger said, the state courts
really never considered the many reasonable alternatives. For
example, the trial judge could have overridden the rule requiring trial in the immediate vicinity and sent it elsewhere. The
judge could have questioned potential jurors extensively to ensure that only those who had not formed an opinion of the case
were accepted as jurors. The judge could have delayed the trial
a few months to let things quiet down. The judge also could have
imposed a gag order on the police and other official participants
in the case. That is not to say that these alternatives would necessarily have worked in this case, but there was nothing in the
record to suggest that they would have failed, either, and apparently they were never even considered.

Moreover, it was not at all clear that the gag order itself
worked. For one thing, the town was so small that all kinds of
stories could and probably did circulate as rumors, many of them
more unfair to the defendant than anything the papers might
have printed or television might have broadcast. Furthermore,
the order could not prohibit out-of-state papers from printing
whatever they wanted, since the local courts have no jurisdiction
beyond state borders, and those newspapers could be brought into
Nebraska. Also, it is hard to predict what kinds of facts or statements will harm a defendant's case; the press remained free to
publish things that might have been as harmful as those that they
were forbidden to print.

For these reasons alone, the gag order could not constitutionally stand.

There were two other problems besides. One was that the
order prohibited reporting of statements and evidence presented
in an open, public hearing. But the First Amendment will never
prevent the press from publishing what goes on in open court.
"Once a public hearing had been held, what transpired there
could not be subject to prior restraint." Second, the order pro-

hibited publishing "implicative facts." But that is "too vague and too broad" a concept to survive First Amendment principles. No one could know what such facts might be, and the risk of self-censorship, as in other cases we have looked at, would be too high.

The Supreme Court did not specifically say that all gag orders would always be unconstitutional. It is possible, the chief justice said, that someday under aggravated circumstances it might be necessary to gag the press to prevent overwhelming pre-trial publicity.

But it will be hard to show that such circumstances are ever present. In a case the following year, the Court threw out another gag order. This one was issued in Oklahoma to prevent disclosure of the name of a juvenile arrested for murder. Although Oklahoma law requires such names to be kept confidential, there had been a hearing open to the public at which the name was disclosed. In a very short opinion, the Court unanimously ruled that the Oklahoma gag order violated the First Amendment.

# 13.

## *ACCESS TO THE PRESS*

A. J. Liebling, the writer and journalism critic, once quipped that in America there is freedom of the press for the man who owns one. As the cases we have already examined make clear, the First Amendment protects the rights of publishers and editors and broadcasters. They may make decisions about what to publish or broadcast and what not to. Those who are not quoted or reported on are out of luck. This may seem unfair. Individuals have no real way to communicate with large numbers of their fellow citizens—at least no way comparable to the voice of a large newspaper or television network, or even to that of the small-town paper, which may circulate in virtually every home in the community. The publisher and editor and writer will be heard, but others will not be. Shouldn't there be a "right of access" to the press—a legal way to compel the press occasionally to report stories it does not want to or to let others tell their own stories? The answer will emerge from our next two cases.

### THE CASE OF THE OFFENDED CANDIDATE

Pat L. Tornillo, Jr., was the Executive Director of the Classroom Teachers Association, a teachers union in Florida. In the fall of 1972, Tornillo ran for a seat in the Florida House of Representatives. In late September, the Miami *Herald* ran two critical editorials opposing his candidacy. The first read as follows:

> LOOK who's upholding the law!
>
> Pat Tornillo, boss of the Classroom Teachers Association and candidate for the State Legislature in the Oct. 3 runoff election, has denounced his opponent as lacking "the knowledge to be a legislator, as evidenced by his failure to file a list of contributions to and expenditures of his campaign as required by law."
>
> Czar Tornillo calls "violation of this law inexcusable."
>
> This is the same Pat Tornillo who led the CTA strike from February 19 to March 11, 1968, against the school children and taxpayers of Dade County. Call it whatever you will, it was an illegal act against the public interest and clearly prohibited by the statutes.
>
> We cannot say it would be illegal but certainly it would be inexcusable of the voters if they sent Pat Tornillo to Tallahassee to occupy the seat for District 103 in the House of Representatives.

Tornillo was outraged and demanded that the *Herald* print verbatim his replies defending his union and his activities. The *Herald* refused. So Tornillo filed suit in a state court. He pointed to an old Florida "right of reply" statute. That law provided that if a candidate for election is attacked by a newspaper about his personal character or official record, the newspaper must on demand print, free of charge, the candidate's reply. Under the law, the reply had to be placed in as prominent a position in the paper and in the same kind of type as the original charges. Failure to comply with the law was punishable as a misdemeanor.

The trial court refused to issue an injunction commanding the *Herald* to accept the ad. It said that the statute (which had been used only once since 1913 when it was enacted) was unconstitutional. The Florida Supreme Court, however, reversed and ruled that the law did not violate the First Amendment. To the contrary, that court said, the right of reply furthered "the broad societal interest in the free flow of information to the public." Any other result, Tornillo said and the court agreed, would leave Tornillo and other candidates at the mercy of newspapers. Times had changed since colonial days when it was relatively inexpensive to establish a newspaper or to print a book or pamphlet to get a viewpoint across to the public. Today, costs are enormous and there are few alternatives available to a person with no direct access to the pages of a newspaper—especially with an election only ten days away.

But on appeal, the U.S. Supreme Court unanimously reversed and declared right of reply laws to be unconstitutional. Writing for the Court, Chief Justice Burger said: "A responsible press is an undoubtedly desirable goal, but press responsibility is not mandated by the Constitution and like many other virtues it cannot be legislated." Burger rejected the argument that the right of reply law did not really infringe on the "*Herald*'s right to speak because it didn't "prevent the *Herald* from saying anything it wished." Such an argument, the chief justice said, begs the question. The real issue is whether a law can require an editor or publisher to print something the paper does *not* wish to publish. The Florida law "exacts a penalty on the basis of the content of a newspaper." One part of the penalty is the cost in time and money to print the reply and the loss of space that could have been devoted to other news. Given the possibility that during a campaign it would constantly be required to print columns written by candidates, a newspaper "might well conclude that the safe course is to avoid controversy. Such self-censorship under legal threat is banned by the First Amendment."

But even if these costs did not exist, Burger went on to say, the law would still flunk the First Amendment test "because of its intrusion into the function of editors. A newspaper is more than a passive receptacle or conduit for news, comment, and advertising. The choice of material to go into a newspaper, and the decisions made as to limitations on the size of the paper, and content, and treatment of public issues and public officials—whether fair or unfair—constitutes [*sic*] the exercise of editorial control and judgment."

The Tornillo decision means what it says: that government is not to interfere with the contents of newspapers. Freedom of the press is freedom to write and publish. It is not a right to compel others to write for you or to give you space to air your opinions. Though, sadly, the number of newspapers is diminishing, there are many outlets for those determined to be heard—and especially for candidates for office. In the long run, any interference by the government in the process by which opinions and news are aired would be far worse than the problem that Florida set out to cure.

## THE BROADCASTING REPLY CASE

On November 27, 1964, Pennsylvania radio station WGCB, owned by the Red Lion Broadcasting Company, aired a fifteen-minute program by the Reverend Billy James Hargis, a well-known right-wing commentator syndicated on many radio stations throughout the country. On this particular program he attacked a book by Fred J. Cook called *Goldwater—Extremist on the Right* (the show was broadcast less than a month after Senator Barry Goldwater lost the presidential election to Lyndon B. Johnson). Hargis was incensed with the book, which he described as intended "to smear and destroy" Goldwater. As part of his discussion, Hargis made a number of exceedingly hostile remarks about Cook, including the charge that Cook had worked for a communist-affiliated magazine. Cook demanded free air time to reply to Hargis' remarks.

Unlike newspapers, the broadcast media—radio and television—are regulated by the government. The Federal Communications Commission (FCC) has the responsibility of issuing licenses to companies that wish to use the various radio and television frequencies. Such licensing is necessary because there are only a limited number of usable frequencies. During the 1920s it became clear that without regulation few if any stations would ever be heard because an increasing number of broadcasters were operating on the same frequencies and drowning each other out. In addition to its licensing authority, the FCC has the power to issue rules to govern the use of the airwaves.

One of the FCC's rules is called the "Fairness Doctrine." The Fairness Doctrine requires that whenever someone's honesty, character, or integrity has been attacked on the air, he has the right to free time within one week during which to reply to the attack. The Fairness Doctrine also requires the radio or television station that carried the attack to provide the person with a copy of a script or tape recording of the attack. (The rule does not apply, incidentally, to attacks by political candidates or their spokespersons on other political candidates or to attacks arising out of genuine news events—for example, on-the-spot reporting during a strike.)

WGCB refused, however, to abide by the Fairness Doctrine, asserting that it was a violation of the station's First Amendment rights. Cook sued, and the case eventually came to the Supreme Court. In a unanimous decision, the Court sided with Cook and against the radio station. The Fairness Doctrine does not violate the First Amendment, the Court said.

But what is the difference between government interference with a newspaper (not permitted) and with a radio or television station (permitted by this decision)? The critical difference, Justice White wrote for the Court, is that broadcast frequencies are a "scarce resource." Anyone can go out and start a newspaper. There is no law of nature that prevents someone from writing his news down on a piece of paper, duplicating it on any one of many commercial processes, like Xerox or mimeograph, and distributing it wherever he likes. But there is a law of nature that prevents people from doing this on the air: there just are not enough frequencies to go around.

That being the case, it is certainly permissible for the government to regulate the use of the airwaves by issuing licenses. "It would be strange," Justice White said, "if the First Amendment, aimed at protecting and furthering communications, prevented the Government from making radio communication possible by requiring licenses to broadcast and by limiting the number of licenses so as not to overcrowd the [radio] spectrum." That does not mean, however, that those who have the licenses are the "owners" of the airwaves in the usual sense of ownership. The airwaves belong to the public, not to the licensees (the radio or television station owners). "It is the right of the viewers and listeners, not the right of the broadcasters, which is paramount," Justice White declared. In fact, he said, it would be unconstitutional if Congress gave total control of the airwaves to private groups with no responsibility to the public. "There is no sanctuary in the First Amendment for unlimited private censorship operating in a medium not open to all," he said.

The radio station argued, as have newspapers in other cases that we have examined, that forcing broadcasters to give free reply time will lead them to self-censorship. The Court had two answers to this argument. First, while there is a possibility of self-censorship it is at the moment only "speculative." Controversial subjects have appeared on radio and television before and the radio and television networks have indicated that they will continue to air controversies despite the Fairness Doctrine. If it does turn out that the stations shy away from hard-hitting news and analysis, that will be the time, the Court said, to re-examine the Fairness Doctrine. Second, the FCC has legal authority to insist that stations devote "adequate and fair attention to public issues."

Finally, the Court noted, the decision in this case does not mean that it would be constitutional for the FCC to censor the content of programs or to order stations to carry all sorts of programs the stations do not want to broadcast. All that was decided was that the First Amendment does not stand in the way of a requirement that reply time be afforded those who have been attacked on the air.

A subsequent Fairness Doctrine case showed that the right

to reply is a limited one. In 1970 the Democratic National Committee asked the FCC to rule that a radio station could not follow a general policy of refusing to accept paid advertising of important public issues. Many radio and television stations refuse to sell air time to groups wishing to discuss controversial public issues on the ground that the issues are adequately covered on their news programs. The FCC said the Fairness Doctrine does not require stations to accept such ads, and the Committee appealed to the Supreme Court. In 1973 the Court agreed by a 7–2 vote that the First Amendment does not require broadcasters to accept paid editorial advertisements.

# 14.

## DOES THE PRESS
## HAVE SPECIAL
## RIGHTS?

Freedom of the press is the right of every person in America, but there is a regular and relatively small group of people who avail themselves of it daily (or weekly or monthly). These are the journalists (reporters, editors, publishers) who staff the nation's newsrooms and publish daily or weekly newspapers, weekly or monthly magazines, and who broadcast the hourly or daily news reports on radio and television. Under the First Amendment, "press" includes more than our customary newspapers, magazines, and radio and television shows: it also covers all sorts of specialty publications from daily newsletters to randomly issued pamphlets, and it certainly includes the book publishing industry. All of these are equally protected by the First Amendment. But usually when we hear the word "press" we think of the publications and shows that bring us news and editorial opinion on a regular basis.

The press in this sense is frequently an adversary of both government and private institutions. Newspapers and news programs are often the bearers of bad tidings. They poke into situations—from Watergate to conditions in local prisons—that officials from Presidents to wardens would rather have them stay away from. Because the press discloses embarrassing, damaging, and often disheartening news, many people grow angry at the press itself. It is an old story that people turn their anger toward the messenger bringing bad news than toward those who caused it.

It is very tempting, therefore, for government officials and others to fight back. As we saw, the Government tried to prevent newspapers from publishing the Pentagon Papers. When a direct attack against publication proved unsuccessful, the Government during the 1970s found other ways to confront the press.

In this chapter we will consider three current press problems. These problems were not new to the 1970s, but they came up then with more frequency and intensity. They are separate issues, but they are related in one central way. That is the claim by the press that established news organizations have special rights not necessarily shared by individual Americans. The claim is that "freedom of the press," as that phrase is used in the First Amendment, must imply rights of access to information, a privilege not to have to reveal sources, and freedom from police searches of newsrooms. These rights, privileges, and freedoms, journalists say, are their only shield against the government's powerful weapons which are capable of preventing important news from being published and forcing the press to be less diligent than it otherwise would be in going after the news.

So far, as we will see in the next three cases, the press has lost the constitutional battle in the courts. The Supreme Court has declared in many cases that the press has no special rights, that it stands on no higher footing than do individual Americans as far as the First Amendment is concerned.

## THE PRISONERS CASE

The Federal Bureau of Prisons, which operates all prisons run by the federal government, has a rule that prohibits all interviews between journalists and "individual inmates." This regulation applies even to interviews that the prisoner himself requests.

In 1972 a reporter for the Washington *Post* asked the U.S. Attorney General for permission to interview specific prisoners in the prisons at Lewisburg, Pennsylvania, and Danbury, Connecticut. Citing the regulation against such interviews, the attorney general turned down the request. Thereafter, the reporter and the *Post* filed suit against the attorney general. They asked the court to declare that they had a First Amendment right to seek out specific inmates and, if the inmates were willing, to interview them about any subjects they cared to discuss.

The federal district court agreed with the newspaper that an absolute ban on such interviews violates the First Amendment. The attorney general appealed to the U.S. Court of Appeals, where he also lost his case. Only when the prison officials can show a particular reason for denying an interview—the bad behavior of a specific inmate, for example, or special conditions existing at the prison at the time of the requested interview—is such a policy legitimate, the appeals court said. But in a 5–4 decision in 1974, the Supreme Court reversed and decided in favor of the attorney general.

Writing for the majority, Justice Stewart noted that the federal prison visitation policy applied not merely to the press but to the general public as well. Only the families, lawyers, and ministers of the prisoners are entitled to visit on a regular basis. Friends of prisoners have a somewhat more limited right. Beyond this group of people, no one else is allowed to interview prisoners and, said Justice Stewart, the "policy is applied with an even hand to all prospective visitors." Moreover, the prison regulations do give journalists certain rights not shared by the public. For example, press photographers may go to any prison and take pictures of the facilities. During such a tour of any prison, the photographer or accompanying journalist may conduct brief conversations with any prisoner they happen to encounter. Prisoners are permitted to write letters to journalists and their mail is not censored. There is a constant turnover in prisoner population, with "a large group of recently released prisoners who are available to both the press and the general public as a source of information about conditions in the federal prisons." For these reasons, Justice Stewart concluded, the regulations are not intended to cover up conditions in the federal prisons.

Freedom of the press is the right to publish, not the right to gather news, the Court said. It is true that some forms of newsgathering are constitutionally protected. Obviously the government could not pass a law prohibiting reporters from asking most people questions, "for without some protection for seeking out the news, freedom of the press could be eviscerated." Nevertheless, the "Constitution does not . . . require government to accord the press special access to information not shared by members of the public generally. . . . That proposition," Justice Stewart declared, "finds no support in the words of the Constitution or in any decision of this Court."

Dissenting, Justice Douglas pointed out that "prohibition of visits by the public has no practical effect upon their right to know [what is going on in prisons]. . . . The average citizen is most unlikely to inform himself about the operation of the prison system by requesting an interview with a particular inmate with whom he has had no prior relationship. He is likely instead, in a society which values a free press, to rely upon the media for information." Douglas found it ironic for the Court majority to justify the ban on press interviews by saying that the press's rights are the same as the public's. Does that mean, Justice Douglas wondered, that the press could be kept from interviewing any governmental employee by passing a law prohibiting members of the public from doing so? Although some restrictions on prisoner interviews may be necessary, he said, an absolute ban is unjustifiable.

Also dissenting, Justice Powell said that the effect of the ban "is to preclude accurate and effective reporting on prison conditions and grievances. These subjects are not privileged or confidential. The Government has no legitimate interest in preventing newsmen from obtaining the information that they may learn through personal interviews or from reporting their findings to the public. Quite to the contrary, federal prisons are public institutions . . . [and what goes on inside] are all matters of legitimate societal interest and concern. . . . [But] no individual can obtain for himself the information needed for the intelligent discharge of his political responsibilities. . . . In seeking out the news the press therefore acts as an agent of the public at large. . . . [The ban on interviews] substantially impairs the right of the people to a free flow of information and ideas on the conduct of their Government."

The Court's ruling does not mean that the Constitution prohibits the government from letting the press into prisons. It merely says that the government isn't obliged to if it doesn't want to. The danger of the ruling lies in the possibility that government officials will seek to bar the press from other places to which the press historically has had access. Barring the doors to a particular reporter or newspaper would clearly violate the First Amendment; exclusion cannot be used as *punishment*. Whether federal, state, or local governments try to keep reporters out of facilities other than prisons remains to be seen.

### THE CONFIDENTIAL SOURCE CASE

Paul M. Branzburg, a reporter for the Louisville (Kentucky) *Courier-Journal*, was assigned to cover drug use in several Kentucky communities. On November 15, 1969, the *Courier-Journal* published one of his stories describing in detail how two youths synthesized hashish from marijuana and earned five thousand dollars in a three-week period. The article stated that Branzburg had agreed with the subjects of his piece not to reveal their identities. On January 10, 1971, Branzburg published another story on the subject in the *Courier-Journal*. This article said that in order to provide a comprehensive survey of the "drug scene," Branzburg had "spent two weeks interviewing several dozen drug users in the capital city" and seen many of them smoking marijuana. Since making, smoking, and selling marijuana are illegal in Kentucky, Branzburg was summoned to appear before a grand jury to testify to the crimes he had witnessed.

Branzburg appeared before the grand jury, but refused to disclose the names of his informants. He argued that to reveal the names of his sources after assuring them that he would not would "destroy the relationship of trust which he presently enjoys with those in the drug culture. They would refuse to speak to him; they would become even more reluctant than they are now to speak to any newsman; and the news media would thereby be vitally hampered in their ability to cover the views and activities of those involved in the drug culture." Branzburg claimed that his right to protect his sources was contained in the First Amendment. To compel any journalist to disclose his sources, he declared, would seriously jeopardize the ability of investigative reporters to gather and report the news.

This was not a novel claim. Many reporters before Branzburg had asserted the same right and refused to hand over the names of their sources. Having done so, many reporters found themselves in contempt of court and sent to jail for days or weeks for their refusals. But journalists consider it as vital to keep their sources confidential as other professionals do in keeping secret all information obtained from clients.

The law recognizes the right of a lawyer, for example, to keep secret whatever a client tells him or her, even if the information concerns a crime. Similarly, doctors and the clergy have a legal "privilege" against testifying to what they learn during the course of a medical examination or a confession, even if demanded by a jury. Although these "privileges" are not based on the First Amendment, the Supreme Court has upheld the rights of these professionals to keep the confidences of their clients, patients, and penitents.

But it had never before ruled on a similar claim by a journalist to preserve the confidence of his sources. In 1972 the case of Branzburg and that of two other journalists who were making similar arguments came to the High Court. By the close vote of

5–4, the Court ruled in June 1972 that there is no constitutional right to refuse to disclose the names of sources to a grand jury.

In his opinion for the majority, Justice White said that the facts had to be understood for what they were. The cases did not involve a restraint on what the press could publish or an order to publish what the newspapers did not want to publish. Nor was the government asserting that reporters must refrain from using confidential sources. "The sole issue before us," he said, "is the obligation of reporters to respond to grand jury subpoenas [orders to appear] as other citizens do and to answer questions relevant to an investigation into the commission of crime." The Court concluded that every reporter has such an obligation. The law has never recognized the "reporter's privilege," Justice White said, but despite the absence of constitutional protection "the press has flourished."

The journalists argued that press subpoenas had been multiplying during the late 1960s and 1970s as more and more reporters began digging up important stories dealing with matters of crime. This was a time of considerable dissent across the country, owing both to the Vietnam war and to civil rights activities. As a result, they claimed, "mutual distrust and tension between press and officialdom have increased," leading to more governmental attempts to haul reporters before grand juries to testify about their sources.

"These developments, even if true," said Justice White, "are treacherous grounds for a far-reaching interpretation of the First Amendment fastening a nationwide rule on courts, grand juries, and prosecuting officials." To say that reporters could always preserve the confidentiality of their sources would involve the courts in all sorts of delicate questions, such as "Who exactly is a reporter?" Trying to answer all the questions that would be presented would slow down the prosecution of criminal cases and would force courts to consider issues they ought to stay away from.

Moreover, Justice White indicated, the ruling that journalists do not have a privilege to withhold the identity of their sources only applies to cases where grand juries are legitimately looking into crimes. If a grand jury called a journalist before it in bad faith, that would present a "wholly different" question. "Official harassment of the press undertaken not for purposes of law enforcement but to disrupt a reporter's relationship with his news sources would have no justification."

Finally, said Justice White, Congress and the state legislatures may, if they wish, enact laws providing journalists with a "shield" against being questioned about their sources. Although there is no First Amendment privilege against testifying, there can be a *legislative* privilege if the legislature chooses to create one.

In dissent, Justice Stewart observed that "it is obvious that informants are necessary to the news-gathering process as we know it today. If it is to perform its constitutional mission, the press must do far more than merely print public statements or publish prepared handouts. Familiarity with the people and circumstances involved in the myriad background activities that result in the final product called 'news' is vital to complete and responsible journalism."

But without being able to promise confidentiality to his sources, the journalist will not be able to form a "productive relationship" with his informants: "An officeholder may fear his superior; a member of the bureaucracy, his associates; a dissident, the scorn of majority opinion. All may have information valuable to the public discourse, yet each may be willing to relate that information only in confidence to a reporter whom he trusts, either because of excessive caution or because of a reasonable fear of reprisals or censure for unorthodox views." The power of government to subpoena reporters and ask them to disclose their sources will reduce the number of people willing to serve as sources and deter newspapers from printing what they say. This is "self-censorship," Justice Stewart concluded, which the First Amendment does not tolerate.

Since the Branzburg case in 1972, scores of reporters have been called before official bodies and asked to disclose their sources. Most have refused. Some have gone to jail for a time.

Others have availed themselves of state "shield laws" that permit them to remain silent. But the question of confidentiality of sources is far from settled. There still is no *federal* shield law (meaning that the Justice Department can subpoena reporters to testify at federal grand juries).

Also, the Supreme Court ducked the opportunity to consider the question of how far a reporter may go in refusing to answer questions when in fact a shield law exists that says he does not have to testify. The case arose out of a celebrated murder trial in New Jersey. Myron Farber, a reporter for the New York *Times*, dug up evidence that led to the prosecution of a man originally known only as "Dr. X" for killing several patients. His lawyers subpoenaed Farber and his notes. New Jersey has a shield law, however, and Farber and the *Times* asserted that he did not have to testify. But the New Jersey courts ruled, in effect, that the state legislature could not tell the state courts how to conduct their business and that Farber would have to testify anyway. Farber went to jail rather than testify. He appealed to the Supreme Court. Although the Court had said in *Branzburg* that states could enact shield laws to protect reporters, the justices declined to hear the appeal. So Farber stayed in jail until the end of the trial; the case ended when the jury acquitted "Dr. X." To what extent shield laws protect reporters remains an important issue.

### THE NEWSROOM SEARCH CASE

On April 8, 1971, a group of student demonstrators seized the administrative offices of the Stanford University Hospital in California. After several attempts to remove them failed, officers of the Palo Alto police department and Santa Clara County sheriff's department were summoned to the building. As they forced their way into the building, a group of the demonstrators emerged from the other end of the corridor brandishing sticks and clubs, with which they attacked a group of nine police officers. All nine were injured in the melee. There were no police photographers at the scene of the fight and most of the witnesses were at the other end of the long corridor. The officers could identify only two of their assailants, but they did notice someone taking pictures from the other end of the hall.

Two days later, on Sunday, April 11, a special edition of the *Stanford Daily*, the university's student paper, carried stories and photographs of the hospital demonstration and fight. From what the picture captions said, it seemed that a student photographer might have been at one end of the hallway.

Believing that the student photographer might have taken pictures that would enable the police to identify the students who assaulted them, the Santa Clara County district attorney's office obtained a search warrant the next day for an immediate search of the newspaper's offices. A search warrant is an order from a court permitting the police to go onto private property to look for specific things. The warrant stated that the police could look for negatives, film, and pictures showing the events and occurrences at the hospital. The warrant did not state that the police believed any staff member of the *Daily* was in any way involved in the hospital fight.

Later that day the police arrived at the *Daily's* offices and in the presence of some staff members made a thorough search. They looked through the photo labs, filing cabinets, desk drawers, and even wastepaper baskets. They did not open locked drawers or locked rooms. But they did have the opportunity to read notes and correspondence during the search (the staff members later claimed that the police officers had gone beyond the limits of the search warrant; the officers denied that they had, and the dispute was never resolved). In the end, the police found no photographs other than those that had already been published in the paper, and they took nothing from the newspaper's offices.

The following month, the *Daily* and several staff members brought suit against the police officers, the district attorney, the judge who issued the warrant and others. The paper asserted that, among other things, the search had violated its First Amendment rights. They said that the district attorney should have subpoenaed the photographs. The difference between a subpoena and a search warrant is this: with a subpoena, the editors would have to bring the photographs to court; with a search warrant the police could come looking. Since they were not accused of a crime, the student editors said, their newsroom should not be subject to a search. The district attorney responded that the trouble with a subpoena is that it gives time to destroy the evidence that the police are searching for, whereas a search warrant gives the police the element of surprise. To this the editors retorted that the police had no reason to believe that the newspaper staff would have destroyed anything.

The editors also argued that whatever the laws governing the use of search warrants, special considerations are at stake in searches of newspaper offices. If notes, photographs, and other documents in newspaper files are liable to be searched (even though the crimes are not committed by anyone connected with the newspaper), then confidential sources will dry up, reporters will not want to preserve their records, and for these and other reasons the press will feel compelled to resort to self-censorship.

When the case reached the Supreme Court in 1978, a 5–3 majority (Justice Brennan took no part in the case) ruled that the First Amendment does not prohibit such a search of a newspaper office. The chief reason, Justice White said in his opinion for the majority, is that the Fourth Amendment, which governs the use of search warrants, has enough safeguards to prevent abuse. In issuing a search warrant, the judge can adequately protect the interests of the press. By specifying exactly what is to be looked for, the search warrant can prevent policemen from rummaging "at large in newspaper files or [intruding into or deterring] normal editorial and publication decisions."

Dissenting, Justice Stewart (himself a former editor-in-chief of his college newspaper) noted that a search warrant "allows police officers to ransack the files of a newspaper, reading each and every document until they have found the one named in the warrant, while a subpoena would permit the newspaper itself to produce only the specific documents requested." The ability to search through all files would mean that it would be very difficult for the press to maintain the confidentiality of their sources. Justice Stewart disagreed with the majority's belief that the judge issuing the warrant could protect confidentiality by specifying exactly what is to be looked for, because in order to *find* the particular things they are looking for the police could plausibly argue that they would have to read each document until they found those they wanted.

"Perhaps as a matter of abstract policy a newspaper office should receive no more protection from unannounced police searches than, say, the office of a doctor or the office of a bank," Justice Stewart said. "But we are here to uphold a Constitution. And our Constitution does not explicitly protect the practice of medicine or the business of banking from all abridgement by government. It does explicitly protect the freedom of the press."

The *Stanford Daily* case drew angry cries from the nation's news organizations. In April 1979, President Carter announced that he would ask Congress to enact legislation to prevent searches such as happened at the offices of the *Daily*. Under the proposed law, courts would be required to subpoena the evidence they wish, allowing editors either to go through their own files or to contest the subpoena in court without outsiders making surprise searches of their newsrooms.

The rulings of the Supreme Court against the press that we have examined in this chapter have worried many thoughtful observers. Despite the statements of several justices that treating the press like any individual will not affect the traditional ability of newspapers and radio and television stations to gather and disseminate the news, there are signs that government officials and private citizens are taking unfair advantage of the opportunities presented by these rulings. Most importantly, many private lawyers on behalf of their clients have been asking for the notes of reporters. According to statistics recently compiled, there were only a dozen subpoenas for reporters' notes between 1960 and 1968. By 1970 about 150 had been issued. From then until 1976 about 500 were issued. The number is now said to be running at 100 a year. Quite aside from the intrusion on the privacy of the press that this implies, the mere act of responding to these subpoenas and of challenging them is becoming an expensive burden.

The failure of the Supreme Court to support the press on these issues does not mean that the press can never have the rights it seeks. Congress and the state legislatures have the power to enact laws restraining the government from interfering with the gathering and the publication of the news. Whether Congress and the state legislatures will do so remains one of the big unanswered questions facing us in the 1980s.

# 15.

## *YOU BE THE JUDGE*

Now that you have read this far, you know quite a bit about the First Amendment. Let's test that knowledge out on some more real Supreme Court cases. First the facts of each case will be set out. If you were the judge, which way would you rule? What reasons would you give?

The answers that the Supreme Court gave are given beginning on page 146. But don't look ahead; try to reason out the answers first yourself. Remember, too, that the answer need not be the final answer. One of the strengths of our legal system is that courts, like the people they are composed of, can change their minds.

### THE "FOR SALE" SIGN CASE

Linmark Associates, a real estate company, decided to sell some property in the township of Willingboro, New Jersey. In 1974 the company listed its property with a real estate agent. The agent wished to place a "For Sale" sign on the lawn of the property. But Willingboro had passed a local ordinance prohibiting the use of "For Sale" and "Sold" signs on private property. The reason for the ordinance was the fear that homeowners were engaged in "panic selling": with a 5% drop in white population and a 60% increase in black population (in 1973 the black population of Willingboro was 18.2%), many whites feared that property values would plummet due to fears that the township was becoming all black. The theory behind the ordinance was that without a sign on the front of the property, it would take much longer to sell each home. The delays would, it was hoped, stop the "panic selling."

Linmark Associates went to court to enjoin the township from enforcing its ordinance and to get a judicial declaration that the ordinance was unconstitutional. The township responded that all it was doing was regulating the manner of offering a home for sale and that the only restriction was on one method of communication.

How should the Court rule?

### THE LICENSE PLATE CASE

The State of New Hampshire issues license plates that bear the motto "Live Free or Die." A state law makes it a misdemeanor to cover up any letters on a motor vehicle license plate. George and Maxine Maynard, Jehovah's Witnesses, found the state motto repugnant to their religious, moral, and political beliefs and covered up the four words that offended them. On three separate occasions George Maynard was arrested for doing so. The first time he was fined twenty-five dollars, but the judge said he would not have to pay during "good behavior." However, Maynard persisted in keeping the motto covered up, and the second time he was convicted he was fined fifty dollars and sentenced to six months in jail. The judge suspended the jail sentence and ordered Maynard to pay the first fine. As a matter of conscience, Maynard said, he would pay neither fine. As a result, he was jailed for fifteen days. The third time he was arrested was before his second trial, and he received no separate punishment.

Since Maynard intended to keep his license plate motto

covered up, he went to court to enjoin the State from prosecuting him further and to get a judicial declaration that the ordinance violated his First Amendment rights. The State responded that the ordinance served two important state interests: (1) the motto "facilitated the identification of passenger vehicles" (making it easier to distinguish New Hampshire cars from out-of-state cars), and (2) the motto "promotes appreciation of history, individualism, and state pride." Does Maynard have a First Amendment right to prevent display of the motto, or are New Hampshire's interests strong enough to overcome any constitutional right Maynard may have?

## THE LAWYER ADVERTISING CASE

John R. Bates and Van O'Steen, two young Arizona lawyers, decided to advertise the services of their law office, which they called a "legal clinic." So they took out an advertisement in the Arizona *Republic*, a daily newspaper in the Phoenix metropolitan area. *"Do You Need a Lawyer?"* the ad asked, answering that the Legal Clinic of Bates & O'Steen provided "legal services at very reasonable fees." It then listed several specific types of services the lawyers would perform and the fees they would charge—for example, adoption, for which they would charge $225. A rule of the Arizona Supreme Court, which has the power to discipline lawyers who violate the profession's code of ethics, prohibited any advertising by lawyers. Although a local lawyers' committee at first suggested that they be suspended from practice for six months, the state supreme court said that they had taken out the ad in a sincere attempt to test the constitutionality of the advertising ban and reduced their punishment to "censure." But the court said that the prohibition against lawyer advertising did not violate the First Amendment because, unlike the situation in the drug price advertising case (p. 85), the advertising of lawyers' services are "inherently" misleading.

The exact services to be performed depend on the individual circumstances in each case. Bates and O'Steen appealed their censure to the Supreme Court. How should the justices rule?

## THE CLOSED COURTROOM CASE

In July 1976, forty-two-year-old Wayne Clapp of Henrietta, New York, a suburb of Rochester, disappeared. After a search, the police discovered that a boat in which Clapp had been fishing the day he disappeared was full of bullet holes. The police then tracked down his two fishing companions, and they were charged with murder. The Rochester *Democrat & Chronicle* and the Rochester *Times-Union*, both owned by the Gannett Company, published a series of articles on Clapp's disappearance and the capture of the suspects. The papers printed eighteen stories between July 20 and August 6, when the suspects were indicted. The stories were straightforward, reporting the facts of the disappearance, the arrests, and certain legal proceedings. From August 6 until November 4, the papers carried no stories on the case at all. During this period, the suspects sought to have statements they made to the police suppressed on the grounds that they had been given involuntarily. They also sought to have evidence excluded from the case on the grounds that it had been unlawfully seized.

Their motions to suppress came before Judge Daniel A. DePasquale at a pre-trial hearing on November 4. The lawyers for the suspects asked that members of both the public and the press be excluded from the courtroom because the buildup of adverse publicity had already prejudiced their clients, and any further reporting would only make the situation worse. The district attorney did not object. A Gannett reporter, Carol Ritter, was present in the court and did not object when the judge closed the courtroom. The next day, however, Ritter wrote to the court and asserted a right "to cover this hearing." Judge DePasquale responded that the hearing had already been held and that he would not immediately release the transcript. The case was appealed. The New York Court of Appeals, the highest state court, ruled that although criminal trials are normally open to the public, including the press, an exception had to be made in this case because of the danger that the publicity would interfere with the suspects' right to a fair trial. On appeal, how should the Supreme Court rule?

### THE HYDROGEN BOMB CASE

Howard Morland, a thirty-six-year-old freelance writer for *The Progressive*, a small magazine of about 60,000 circulation nationally, wrote an article entitled "How the Hydrogen Bomb Works." *The Progressive* commissioned the article in order to show that from facts available to anyone who wishes to do some honest research, it is possible to figure out how to build a hydrogen bomb. Morland, whose technical background consisted of several college courses in chemistry and physics, spent six months doing his research. Morland neither stole any documents nor had any unauthorized access to classified documents. Finding out about the article, the Justice Department went to court to enjoin *The Progressive* from publishing it.

This case, the Government said, was one of those rare instances in which it was permissible to engage in prior restraint of the press. The Supreme Court said as long ago as 1931 in the Near case (p. 22) that certain kinds of information, like troop movements and sailing dates of ships in wartime, could be censored. This was such a case, the Government said. Imagine the consequences of a foreign government's reading the article and then building the bomb to terrorize its neighbors. In order to avoid that, the Justice Department said, the article must be stopped.

To Morland's argument that he had gotten all his information legally and from material that was already public, the Government replied that certain kinds of information about atomic energy are "classified at birth." What the Government meant is that certain kinds of information are so dangerous that the Government has the right to restrict them from the moment they are discovered or invented.

Should the Government win its case?


## WHAT THE JUDGES SAID


### THE "FOR SALE" SIGN CASE

Linmark Associates won its case. In a unanimous decision the Court said that the township's interest in promoting stable, racially integrated housing, while vitally important, does not outweigh the right of its citizens to receive information. The township was not regulating the manner of expression at all, but the content, and this it may not do under the First Amendment. "If dissemination of this information can be restricted, then every locality in the country can suppress any facts that reflect poorly on the locality." But the Virginia drug price advertising case "denies government such sweeping powers."


### THE LICENSE PLATE CASE

Maynard won his case. In a 7–2 decision, the Court said that "the First Amendment protects the right of individuals to hold a point of view different from the majority and to refuse to foster, in the way New Hampshire commands, an idea they find morally objectionable."


### THE LAWYER ADVERTISING CASE

Bates and O'Steen won their case. By a 5–4 vote, the Court ruled that there was nothing inherently deceptive about the ad. The lawyers made no claims about the *quality* of their services— such a claim might be inherently misleading, because how can quality of a lawyer's services or performance be measured? But all Bates and O'Steen did was to state actual charges for simple services that are quite routine. Indeed, the Arizona State Bar Association itself sponsored a program in which the very services that Bates and O'Steen promised to perform were made available to consumers at standardized rates. This decision does not mean that states may not regulate attorney advertising, only that states may not "prevent the publication in a newspaper of a truthful advertisement concerning the availability of routine legal services."

### THE CLOSED COURTROOM CASE

By a 5–4 vote, the Supreme Court ruled that the press did not have a right to cover the pre-trial hearing. In the majority opinion, Justice Stewart noted that the Sixth Amendment to the Constitution guarantees to a defendant the right to a "public trial." Such a right belongs to the defendant only, Justice Stewart said, and not to the public or to the press. Although "there is no question that the Sixth Amendment permits and even presumes open trials," it does not *require* them, Justice Stewart said. If the defendant and the prosecutor agree to a non-public trial, the judge may close the courtroom. There is no right given to the press by the First Amendment to attend judicial proceedings.

In a long dissent, Justice Blackmun sought to show that the Court majority misread the history of public trials before the Sixth Amendment was written and that it was not the intent of the drafters of the Sixth Amendment to give a defendant the right whenever he wants to close a trial. Moreover, said Justice Blackmun, the public has a very real interest in having access to criminal trials to assure that the court remains impartial and that the actions of public officials in the case were lawful. A closed trial might permit the prosecutor to cover up wrongdoing, just as it would permit the defendant to have his wrongdoing go unrecorded in detail.

It is interesting to note that within the first five weeks after the Court's decision on July 2, 1979, lawyers in thirty-nine cases requested that courtrooms be cleared of the public or the press, and in twenty-one of those cases the judges agreed to do so. In one case, the judge said reporters would have to leave the courtroom but he permitted members of the public to stay. The following month, four justices of the Court suggested in public speeches that lower court judges may have misread the opinion. It is exceedingly rare for a single justice to make remarks outside the Court about one of its decisions and for four justices to do so is unprecedented, so it is quite likely that we have not heard the final word on this controversy.

### THE HYDROGEN BOMB CASE

A Michigan trial judge granted the government's request for an injunction against publishing the story. This was said to be the first time in American history that a federal court had enjoined publication of a news article. The trial judge said that it would be better to err against *The Progressive* than against the government, for if the government was right in its claim that publication of the article could be tremendously dangerous to the security of the nation and the world, then a decision to let the magazine publish the article would, as a practical matter, be the end of the case. Once the article was published, there would be no way for a higher court to reverse the decision. However, during the months after the judge temporarily enjoined the publication of the article, the magazine's lawyers were able to show that much of the material the government was afraid might become public had been freely available in various libraries. Then, as the case was appealed to a U.S. Court of Appeals, another small periodical printed a letter from an engineer covering much of the material that Morland had developed in his article. Since the information had thus become public, the government decided to drop its suit, leaving *The Progressive* free to publish the Morland piece.

# A FINAL WORD

We began with the words, "It's a free country!" Having now explored some fifty cases interpreting and applying the charter of our basic liberties, we can see that the forty-five simple words of the First Amendment are only the beginning of freedom, not the end. It should be clear by now why the constitutional command that the government stay out of our thoughts, opinions, and the way we express them so often figures in court cases. People who do not respect the Constitution's commands must be brought to court; people who do not understand its requirements must be given explanations; people who have forgotten must be reminded.

It should also be clear by now—and may perhaps be a little astonishing—how broad a spectrum of cases has come to court. The constitutional guarantees of free speech and free press touch many spheres of life and many activities of men and women, children and students, because so much of our civilization revolves around thought and expression. This is not accidental. It is part and parcel of being human.

The First Amendment is a great and good thing. But so bright is its constitutional radiance that it sometimes blinds people to another great truth. To the First Amendment, as Justice Powell put it, "there is no such thing as a false idea." That is true as far as it goes, and it is an important truth. It means that the *government* may not discriminate among ideas, telling us which ideas we may consider and which we may not, what we may say or print and what we may not, what is safe to talk about and what is not.

But the First Amendment does not mean that we as *individuals* may not regard some ideas as false. Indeed, it leaves us free to do exactly that. Ideas are not all equal. To hold that the government and law must tolerate all ideas does not also mean that as individuals we must do so. There are ideas of hate as well as love, of harm as well as safety, of nonsense as well as intelligence. As individuals, we must learn to distinguish between them, rejecting the former and accepting the latter. No one will make us do it. But we are free to do it. That is the lesson of the First Amendment.

# GLOSSARY

APPEAL—a request to a higher or appellate court to review the decision made in a trial or lower court.

BILL OF RIGHTS—the first ten amendments to the U.S. Constitution.

BREACH OF PEACE—a public disturbance.

CLEAR AND PRESENT DANGER—a test devised by Justice Holmes for punishing people for their speech or writing despite the First Amendment: if the speech presents an obvious and immediate danger to an important governmental interest (such as conduct of a war), then the speaker may be punished.

CONSTRUE—interpret; discern the meaning of a statute.

CONTEMPT—the act of violating a court order.

DEFAMATION—any type of injury to a person's reputation.

DEFENDANT—a person who is prosecuted by the state in a criminal case; the person who is sued for money damages or an injunction in a civil case.

DISCRETION—the power a judge has to decide delicate questions on his own; normally when a judge exercises his discretion an appellate court will not reverse his use of discretion.

ENJOIN—what a court does when it orders someone to cease doing something; the order is called an "injunction."

FAIRNESS DOCTRINE—a rule of the Federal Communications Commission requiring broadcasters to give free air time to persons whose character or honesty is attacked on the air.

FIGHTING WORDS—hostile remarks, directed toward particular individuals, that are highly likely to provoke a breach of the peace.

GAG ORDER—a court order prohibiting various people from discussing a pending case; also, an order to a newspaper or broadcaster not to publish or broadcast.

INJUNCTION—a court order prohibiting a person from taking a specific act; violation of an injunction is punishable as a contempt of court.

INHERENT POWER—the doctrine that a governmental body, such as a court, has the legal authority to take a certain action even if there is no specific law permitting it to do so.

LIBEL—a written defamation.

LOYALTY OATH—a statement, either oral or in writing, that a person (usually a government employee) will remain loyal to the state or federal government.

MALICE—generally, ill-will; in the First Amendment sense, the act of libeling or slandering with the knowledge that the statement was false or with reckless disregard for the likelihood that it was false.

ORDINANCE—a law passed by a local government such as a town.

PICKET—the act of demonstrating against an employer or some other entity.

PLAINTIFF—the person or party who files a lawsuit.

PRECEDENT—a case already decided that states a legal principle to be followed in future cases with similar facts.

PRIOR RESTRAINT—an injunction or other means of preventing publication.

PUBLIC FIGURE—a person who is in the public eye but who does not hold public office.

PUBLIC OFFICIAL—a person who holds public office; a government employee.

RIGHT TO REPLY LAW—a law giving a person attacked the right to give his or her side of the controversy.

SEARCH WARRANT—an order of a court giving police or similar officials the right to search through private property to look for evidence of a crime or for the criminal.

SEDITION—an act of inciting hostility toward or rebellion against a government.

SEDITIOUS LIBEL—statements that scorn, ridicule, or hold in contempt a particular government.

SHIELD LAW—a law that gives a reporter or other writer a privilege against testifying as to the identity of his sources in court or at another official hearing.

SLANDER—oral defamation.

STAY—an order of a court preserving the status quo until a ruling can be made.

STATUTE—a law enacted by a legislature, as opposed to a rule announced by a court or a regulation adopted by an administrative agency such as the Federal Communications Commission.

SYMBOLIC SPEECH—an act that expresses an idea.

# FOR FURTHER READING

Hundreds of books and thousands of articles have been written about the First Amendment and its freedoms. Of these, two of the best and most enduring are:

Zechariah Chafee, Jr. *Free Speech in the United States,* Atheneum, 1961. (Originally published by Harvard University Press, 1941.)
Thomas I. Emerson. *The System of Freedom of Expression,* Random House, 1970.

The following books are of special interest in the categories listed:

COLONIAL HISTORY:

Leonard W. Levy. *Freedom of Speech and Press in Early American History: Legacy of Suppression,* Harper Torchbooks, 1963.
Leonard W. Levy, ed. *Freedom of the Press from Zenger to Jefferson, Early American Libertarian Theories,* Bobbs-Merrill Co., Inc., 1966. (A collection of fascinating historical documents.)

GENERAL HISTORIES:

William L. Chenery. *Freedom of the Press,* Harcourt Brace, 1955.
John Hohenberg. *Free Press/Free People, the Best Cause,* Columbia University Press, 1971.

CURRENT ISSUES:

Fred P. Graham. *Press Freedoms Under Pressure,* The Twentieth Century Fund, 1972.

Benno C. Schmidt, Jr. *Freedom of the Press vs. Public Access,* Praeger, 1976.

Fred W. Friendly. *The Good Guys, The Bad Guys, and the First Amendment,* Random House, 1976.

Howard Simons and Joseph A. Califano, Jr., eds. *The Media and the Law,* Praeger, 1976. (Includes full transcripts of fascinating dialogues among lawyers, judges, reporters, and editors on some of the issues discussed in this book.)

Those who would like to read about current legal issues on a regular basis should subscribe to *The News Media and the Law,* a magazine published six times a year by The Reporters Committee for Freedom of the Press. (Write to Reporters Committee, 1750 Pennsylvania Avenue N.W., Room 1112, Washington, D.C. 20026.)

# TABLE OF CASES

The following are the names and legal citations for the cases discussed in each chapter. If you wish to read the judges' opinions for yourself, a librarian in any law library will easily locate the cases for you.

CHAPTER 3
*Near v. Minnesota,* 283 U.S. 697 (1931).
*New York Times Company v. United States,* 403 U.S. 713 (1971).

CHAPTER 4
*Schenck v. United States,* 249 U.S. 47 (1919).
*Abrams v. United States,* 250 U.S. 616 (1919).
*Taylor v. Mississippi,* 319 U.S. 583 (1943).
*Bond v. Floyd,* 385 U.S. 116 (1966).
*De Jonge v. Oregon,* 299 U.S. 353 (1937).
*Dennis v. United States,* 341 U.S. 494 (1951).
*Yates v. United States,* 354 U.S. 298 (1957).
*Scales v. United States,* 367 U.S. 203 (1961).

CHAPTER 5
*Chaplinsky v. New Hampshire,* 315 U.S. 568 (1941).
*Terminiello v. Chicago,* 337 U.S. 1 (1949).
*Feiner v. New York,* 340 U.S. 315 (1951).
*Thornhill v. Alabama,* 310 U.S. 88 (1940).
*Cox v. Louisiana,* 379 U.S. 536, 379 U.S. 559 (1965).

CHAPTER 6

*United States v. O'Brien,* 391 U.S. 367 (1968).

*Spence v. Washington,* 418 U.S. 405 (1974).

*Tinker v. Des Moines Independent Community School District,* 393 U.S. 503 (1969).

CHAPTER 7

*West Virginia State Board of Education v. Barnette,* 319 U.S. 624 1943).

*Elfbrandt v. Russell,* 384 U.S. 11 (1966).

CHAPTER 8

*Schneider v. Irvington,* 308 U.S. 147 (1939).

*Martin v. City of Struthers,* 319 U.S. 141 (1943).

*Breard v. Alexandria,* 341 U.S. 622 (1951).

*Saia v. New York,* 334 U.S. 558 (1948).

*Kovacs v. Cooper,* 336 U.S. 77 (1949).

*Lovell v. Griffin,* 303 U.S. 444 (1938).

*Valentine v. Chrestensen,* 316 U.S. 52 (1942).

CHAPTER 9

*Bigelow v. Virginia,* 421 U.S. 809 (1975).

*Virginia State Board of Pharmacy v. Virginia Citizens Consumer Council, Inc.,* 425 U.S. 748 (1976).

*Federal Trade Commission v. Colgate-Palmolive Co.,* 380 U.S. 374 (1965)

CHAPTER 10

*New York Times v. Sullivan,* 376 U.S. 254 (1964).

*Garrison v. Louisiana,* 379 U.S. 64 (1964).

*Gertz v. Robert Welch, Inc.,* 418 U.S. 323 (1974).

*Cox Broadcasting Corp. v. Cohn,* 420 U.S. 469 (1975).

CHAPTER 11

*Joseph Burstyn, Inc., v. Wilson,* 343 U.S. 495 (1952).

*Roth v. United States,* 354 U.S. 476 (1957).

*Memoirs v. Massachusetts,* 383 U.S. 413 (1966).

*Stanley v. Georgia,* 394 U.S. 557 (1969).

*Miller v. California,* 413 U.S. 15 (1973).

# INDEX